The Pocket

Handbook

to Life

Solutions

Original Published by:

Genesis Life 55 Books™

D. R. McGregor - 2024

Christchurch,

New Zealand

ISBN: 978-1-7386119-2-8

Genesis
Life 55 Books™

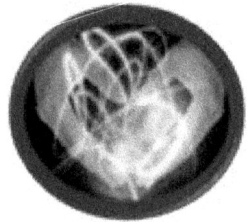

Be honest with those close to you,

For the biggest challenge in your existence called life,

Is to be honest with oneself.

- **D. R. McGregor** -

By

D.R. McGregor

We Pray to Die – A Convict's True Story
(Revised Edition)

Martin Bryant – Guilty or Not Guilty?
'A Review of The Crime – 28 Years On'

The Story Behind a Massacre
(Limited Availability)

We Pray to Die – A Convict's Story

The Life Handbook of Challenges

'The Challenge of Life'

A journey of self-understanding and self-development,

To be as one with the World, the Universe

And the life you live.

Whether it's praise, love, criticism, money, time, power, punishment, space, sorrow, laughter, need, pain, or pleasure... the more of it that you give, the more of it you will receive.

Please Note:

Some areas of this book may sound repetitive;
To think positive, change a habit, and living life
To achieve your goals and dreams is a
Repetitive process.

For My Family

This bright, new day
Complete with 24 hours of opportunities,
Choices and attitudes, a perfectly matched
set of 1440 minutes.
86400 perfectly timed seconds any of
which cannot be wasted.
This unique gift, this one day, cannot be exchanged,
replaced or refunded. Handle with care.
Make the most of it.
There is only one to a customer.

The Following Will Give You Inspiration Daily

What Happens   What is Achieved

What Happens	What is Achieved
Laziness **Kills** *Ambition*	*Ambition* **Kills** Laziness
Anger **Kills** *Wisdom*	*Wisdom* **Kills** *Anger*
Fear **Kills** *Dreams*	*Dreams* **Kill** *Fear*
Jealousy **Kills** *Peace*	*Peace* **Kills** *Jealousy*
Doubt **Kills Confidence**	*Confidence* **Kills** *Doubt*

'Anonymous'

"There is no use whatever trying
to help people who do not help themselves. You cannot
push anyone up a ladder unless he be willing to climb
himself".

'Andrew Carnegie'

'Everyone needs a tool kit for your life'

Nobody ever said it would be easy, right? But why are there so many fancy words for such a simple idea? Self-improvement, personal-development, self-empowerment, neurolinguistic programming, behaviour modification, self-fulfilment, perfecting your human potential, strengthening your interpersonal communication skills . . . Talk!

The bottom line is you want to make things better. On the other hand, if everything in your life is terrific, you may wonder every now and then, just a fleeting thought, if it can last. But you know the answer to that, nothing is frozen in time. Things change.

They get better, or they get something else. The point is you want to have some control over which way things go in your life. But the only thing in life that you truly have control over is yourself.

You will not change anyone in this world, all you can do is work towards changing **YOU**.

So that's where you start. Decide what you want to do and take one step in that direction. Then another, and in the perfectly natural way of things, one thing leads to another one step leads to another and you change.

You change the world around you. Nope, nobody said it would be easy. But it shouldn't be so hard to start.

1

Look inside, explore this book and all it has to offer. If you don't see what you need, what have you lost nothing but a little time to read?

But the first step is simply deciding that you want to take the first step. Your thoughts, your dreams, your intentions are the power of the Universe! Then, just Imagine what you can do. You have incredible powers that can change your life use those powers and **'JUST DO IT'.**

Here are some of the benefits you'll enjoy in just a few days of working with the tools and ideas from this handbook:

- Develop Positive Thinking
- Create Powerful Affirmations
- End Stress
- Take Control of Your Life
- Create Fulfilling Relationships
- Improve Your Finances
- End Fear
- Boost Your Creativity
- Increase Self Confidence
- Stop Worrying
- End Negative Thinking
- Enjoy Inner Peace
- Succeed in Business

- Enjoy Better Health
- Meet the Perfect Partner
- End Negative Feelings
- Take Charge of Your Life
- Get a Better Job
- Secure a Promotion
- Create and alter situations to what you want.

I appreciate better than most the challenges you face but let's face it, life is full of challenges!

Introduction

In your day-to-day activities there are so many challenges that are thrust upon us. Do we back off from them, or face them with the human spirit that is an Instinct? For some of us to even get up from our beds in the morning, to eat breakfast or even go to work is a challenge. Let us firstly consider the word *'Challenge'*, what does this really mean in terms of our everyday lives.

The most common interpretation is;
   'A contest against one's opponents, a test of abilities and strength, also the knowledge and skill to complete the task'.

Looking carefully at these, why do we even create or bring challenges upon ourselves? The overall picture of our lives, it is my belief and that of some very well-educated people that we need to have five main items or instincts to our being, just like our five main senses. Each of these instincts and senses, need to be present for us to face every day of our lives.
Should one of them be missing then our whole persona is thrown off and we are unable to function fully as a human being.

Please understand here I do not in any way mean that a person with a deficiency is unable to function fully because they are missing one of their senses, they compensate and they have a challenge created for them which through their abilities, knowledge and skill live a perfectly normal life.

Persons with the loss of sight or hearing or one of the other main senses are of greater strength and ability than the person who has all fully functional senses.

They have a challenge every living moment of their existence and therefore can create solutions to any problem or situation which arises. They do not have a challenge to be able to see or hear as their ability and inner strength, to step up and face the world no matter what is dealt to them is ongoing.

In 1996 I came up with a format for myself to start to try and goal orientate my life, considering the challenges I had already faced and what was to be my future. I wrote the following down and have used this to this day as a basis for how I solve problems and to turn a challenge into a positive. For all negatives there must be a positive for the world to go ahead, as it is with life, turn a negative into a positive and use it to advantage. Using the five senses and instincts as shown, I place the challenge into one of the categories and then look for the positive from that.

Our Five senses we talk about are:

- Touch (Feel),

- Smell.
- Sight,
- Hearing,
- Taste

My Five instincts I talk about are:

- Life,
- Gratitude,
- Love,
- Humanity,
- Wisdom.

I have paired up my *Instinct*s with the *Senses* that I believe match.

So, we have :-

- *Life is Sight* -   What life reveals to us by being able to view the marvels of our existence whether we can see it or not is a challenge in itself.
- *Gratitude is Taste* – We are grateful for the food and sustenance provided to us which helps us to survive and have the strength to face the challenges in life.

- *Love is Touch* - To touch something is to gain an understanding and either a love or resentment for that item.

- *Humanity is Hearing* – To be able to hear a compliment or thanks, is a human feeling we all look for at some point.

- *Wisdom is Smell* – We at some point have used the phrase, *"I smell a rat"* so using our sense of smell we used wisdom to decipher what the problem *(the rat)* was or is.

From the above we can now advance our understanding more of how our instincts combined with our senses influence us in everyday life. Our senses help us to survive and learn, our instincts teach us to develop and grow.

Albert Einstein wrote - *"A human being is a part of the whole called by us the Universe, a part limited in time and space. He experiences himself, his thoughts, and feelings as something separated from the rest, a kind of optical delusion of his consciousness. This delusion is a kind of prison for us, restricting us to our personal desires and to affection for a few persons nearest to us. Our task must be to free ourselves from this prison by widening our circle of compassion to embrace all living creatures and the whole of nature in its beauty.* "

****

So, for one to be at peace, your instincts and senses must be as one and combine to enhance our being and what our world and life has to offer. This book is by no means the be all and end all of solutions. It is what I now live by and what has helped me survive the challenges and obstacles placed before me. We are on this planet in this time to learn a lesson and to contribute some small part to the existence of humanity. I am a believer that we have all lived earlier lives and for the same reasons we had to learn lessons and practice those lessons.

A greater power has pre-determined our past, present and future and for this reason I believe I have found my calling and my lesson learnt to pass this on to others and to teach how our senses and instincts when in harmony help us to create a better and more fulfilling life, not only for ourselves and those close to us but even for those we do not even know.

To pass on knowledge and any lessons learnt whilst on this wonderful journey of life and existence is the fulfilment and satisfaction that you can receive both mentally and physically. I now invite you to read my story and hopefully understand what it meant to me to realise my potential and hopefully help you to understand how you may be able to overcome,

"The Challenge".

Do Not think about what you are going to do, *Just Do It.* Being human is itself difficult, and therefore all kinds of challenges create problems!

The Author's Challenges

Well, you might say, why do we need to know the ins and outs of the Author's life, we all have had problems of one sort or another. I agree fully that you should feel like this. But for me to truly show you in this book, how I changed my life around and changed my thought processes I believe that maybe just maybe, I have had a little more than the average person. I also took this as a negative believing that I am a slow learner and cannot perceive what right I have on this earth and why does the

Almighty keep causing me these horrendous health problems.

What I am really trying to say is that I am by no means alone in having such challenges in my short existence, and I am sure there are many worse off than myself. But have they sat and tried to understand or correlate why? This is why I have spread my life as an open book to show that each hurdle placed in front of me, I found a solution, a plan if you like, to resurrect my life to get on and be the person I believe I should be. We as said are put here to learn lessons, some faster than others, some are slow learners, then there are the ones who cannot learn or the people who just refuse to open and learn.

This book I realise will not help everyone, it may not help anyone at all, but if all that read it take a small piece of my philosophy and use it for their advantage and it helps them to face their demons and challenges then I have succeeded and another part of my journey has been completed.

My real challenges started in 1975, when I was injured in a work accident and my left leg was damaged. The first of many operations to correct the problem started a snowball effect which as you will read on becomes a nightmare. I tore a Medial Ligament, which needed to be worked on. I was given a drug to help with the recovery, I continued to take this tablet as prescribed for a period when again I injured the knee. Again, it was necessary to operate and again I was prescribed the same drug; which reacted severely with me and caused acute stomach and bowel problems. (I will not go into all the medical terms as I believe it unnecessary).

This led to a major operation of almost twelve hours to correct the problem which the medication had caused. Ten days after the operation it was discovered that a set of ten-inch forceps (Medical clamps) had been left inside of me. Back to the operating theatre, another four- and half-hour operation. After this, I was assuming all would be okay and that I could now get on with my life as normal as possible. One should never assume, ten weeks later my Appendix burst inside of me and another five-hour operation to remove and hopefully, finally, cure me. Was I now in the clear? One would hope so.

Three months to the day of my Appendix operation, I was back in hospital again, my Gall Bladder had failed and had to be removed. After this operation, the mind and body did not want anymore. During this period, my first wife walked out on me and left me for another man. I could not blame her, I had spent almost two thirds of our married life in hospital, so she needed to be free to lead a normal life. I had had enough, the greatest challenge I thought at the time was upon me. I had no home, no real outlook, felt like the bottom of sewer drain. I felt like there was nothing left for me, either in my life or inside to remove. Was I ever wrong!

Next, I developed a problem with reflux due to all the operations and having the stomach and my insides basically removed and replaced so many times over a brief period. It was I am sure nature saying this has got to be put right and all back in the right place. After a period of almost 3 years of tests and a pharmacy full of different drugs to try and correct the problem, another challenge was thrown at me. I contracted Viral Meningitis, this I believed was the end, my body and my sanity could take no more.

Depression fell heavily upon my soul and my full belief in God and the Universe has a reason for us existing, went out the window. I had no beliefs, no truth to my own being and why I was being put to so many tests and still had no clear view of what my future held. It was during this stay in hospital that they also discovered a blood problem which has a near unpronounceable name *Immuno-Thrombocytopenia-Purpura,* it is shortened to ITP. Basically, my blood was slow to clot due to a lack of Platelets. My body, I honestly believed was trying to kill itself, I no longer had control of my own destiny. There was a power greater than my heart and soul, trying to make me self-destruct. Repeatedly over and over I asked the question, why?

My intrepid journey continued, I recovered from the Meningitis and hoped with all my heart and soul I was now on the road to a full recovery and that my life would be normal as far as possible, and that I would be able to have some control.

I was joking with myself. Due to the Reflux problem, I then had to have another operation to help slow it down and hopefully correct the problem. The same operation my Spleen was removed to try and help with the ITP. I prayed this would be all that was needed and that I had seen the last of operating theatres. I felt like they had become my second home along with a permanent hospital bed. Little did I know that my real problems were only just beginning? Over the ensuing years I had to have further operations on the left leg to help repair the knee as well as vein problems caused by bad circulation. There are too many operations to list them all that also occurred in between those mentioned. But the hospital stays continued, control of my health was in the hands of others, as was my mind and self-doubt haunted me every waking hour.

I hope now you understand why I share my challenges and I was not finished yet. Life had dealt me a crooked hand and I was to be beaten by the turn of the life cards yet again. I had over the years had a slight tremor in the right hand which also went to my left hand. I put it down to stress and worry from what had happened over the past years and the amount of operations I had undergone. I was to be proven wrong again.

With all that had happened, and still only forty years of age, I was to now develop the symptoms of what many called *"The Old Man's Disease"* Parkinson's disease. This problem I have learnt can affect anyone of any age and be debilitating to the point, where the sufferer cannot walk, talk, or even feed themselves. It has even been described as a *"Living Death Sentence"*.

I am, I suppose a lucky one as I can talk, although at times with difficulty in that I may slur my words, or dribble saliva from the side of my mouth. I can walk with a shuffle and have moments of freezing. I have a tremor, and this is probably the most embarrassing when trying to have a drink or eat, half of the contents can end up down my front or in my lap.

I decided that things had gone too far and needed some help, so I consulted my doctor, who in his wisdom and for which I am thankful for sent me to see a Neurologist. This was one of three Neurologists I was to be examined by and they all diagnosed me with "Parkinson's Disease".

When first informed I felt this was the last straw. I had had too many challenges thrown at me and finally a death sentence. I asked the obvious question, *"How Long?"* the reply *"how long what!!"* The Neurologist went on to explain what it was and that I will live a normal and fulfilling life with the right drugs. I thought to myself here we go again, more drugs, I was like a walking pharmacy now with what I had to take.

Depression and suicidal thoughts were now also causing not only me but my family real concern. I was at my lowest ebb, and the Dark Lord visited often trying to convert me into his way of thinking. I admit, I did finally give to the pressure and in some dark moment of depression I was ready for my maker and gave willing. The problem here I failed, I failed again in life. I had no more will power; I was full of self-doubt and confusion. My pathway in life had had far too many obstacles placed upon it. I was tired and worn out.

My next visit to the Neurologist explained "Parkinson's disease is a disorder that affects nerve cells in the part of the brain controlling muscle movement. People with Parkinson's disease often experience trembling, muscle rigidity, difficulty walking, problems with balance and slowed movements. These symptoms usually develop after age 60, although some people affected by Parkinson's disease are younger than age 50. Parkinson's disease is progressive, meaning the signs and symptoms become worse over time. But although Parkinson's disease may eventually be disabling, the disease often progresses gradually, and most people have many years of productive living after a diagnosis. Furthermore, unlike other serious neurological diseases, Parkinson's disease is treatable. One treatment approach is medications. Another involves an implanted device that stimulates the brain. Other approaches involve surgery.

Meanwhile, research into other treatments continues. PD is both chronic and progressive. PD is the most common cause of Parkinsonism, a group of similar symptoms. PD is also called "Primary Parkinsonism" or "Idiopathic PD" (having no known cause). While most forms of Parkinsonism are Idiopathic, there are some cases where the symptoms may result from toxicity, drugs, genetic mutation, head trauma, or other medical disorders.

The earliest symptom of Parkinson's disease can be as subtle as an arm that doesn't swing when you walk, a mild tremor in the fingers of one hand or soft, mumbling speech that's difficult to understand. You may lack energy, feel depressed or have trouble sleeping. Or you may notice that it takes you longer to shower, shave, eat or do other routine tasks." He slowly explained all this to me and at some point, during this I realised there was a light, some hope, a reason for me being here, all I had to do was find it within myself and then explore it. He continued and I listened with a whole new intention. "There were other signs and symptoms of Parkinson's disease" he explained.

I will now briefly enlighten you on those as with this knowledge, you can come to better understand why I authored this book.

- *Tremor.* This often starts with a slight shaking in your hand or even one finger. Sometimes hand tremor causes a back-and-forth rubbing of your thumb and forefinger known as pill-rolling. Tremor may also develop in your legs. These signs may occur on one or both sides of your body and may be more noticeable when you're under stress. Although tremor can be very distressing, it's usually not disabling and often disappears when you're sleeping. Many people with Parkinson's disease do not experience large tremor.

- *Slowed motion (bradykinesia).* Over time, Parkinson's disease may cause a slow, shuffling walk with an unsteady gait and stooped posture. And leg muscles may freeze up, making it hard to resume normal movement. This is especially distressing because it can make performing the simplest tasks difficult and time-consuming.

- *Rigid muscles.* Muscle stiffness (rigidity) often occurs in your limbs and neck. Sometimes the stiffness can be so severe that it limits the size of your movements and causes pain.

- *Impaired balance.* Your posture may become unstable because of Parkinson's disease. Often this problem is still minor for many years.

- *Loss of automatic movements.* Blinking, smiling, and swinging your arms when you walk are all unconscious acts that are a normal part of being human. In Parkinson's disease, these acts tend to be diminished and even lost. Some people may develop a fixed staring expression and unblinking eyes. Others may no longer gesture or seem animated when they speak.

- *Impaired speech.* Many people with Parkinson's disease have some trouble speaking, and their voices often become monotonous and incredibly soft. This may be a special problem for older adults because the soft voice of a person with Parkinson's disease may not be audible to a spouse with poor hearing.

- *Difficulty swallowing.* This may develop in the later stages of the disease, but except in rare cases, most people who have trouble swallowing can continue to eat on their own.

- *Dementia.* A small percentage of people with Parkinson's develop this mental disorder — which affects the ability to think, reason and remember — late in the course of the disease. Although it's often associated with Alzheimer's disease, dementia can also occur with other conditions. In Parkinson's, the onset of dementia is often marked by slowed thought processes and problems with concentration.

In the nearly 200 years since Parkinson's disease was first described, researchers have come to understand some of the processes of this complex disorder. They now know that many of the signs and symptoms of Parkinson's disease develop when certain nerve cells (neurons) in an area of the brain called the substantia nigra are damaged or destroyed. Normally, these nerve cells release dopamine, a chemical that transmits signals between the substantia nigra and another part of the brain, the corpus striatum. These signals cause your muscles to make smooth, controlled movements. Everyone loses some dopamine-producing neurons as a normal part of aging. But people with Parkinson's disease lose half or more of neurons in the substantia nigra. Although other brain cells also degenerate, the dopamine-containing cells are critical for movement and so take centre stage.

Just what causes this is a subject of intense research. Scientists believe Parkinson's disease may result from a combination of genetic and environmental factors. Certain drugs, diseases and toxins also may cause symptoms like those of Parkinson's disease.

Scientists believe that genes contribute to the development of Parkinson's, but it's not yet clear whether heredity plays a major or minor role in this disease. It has been known for some time that people with a first-degree relative with Parkinson's disease, such as a parent, child, or sibling, are more likely to develop the disease than are people without a family connection. Although the risk among first-degree relatives is small less than 5 percent it nevertheless suggests a genetic link. For that reason, scientists have focused on the rare families in which several people have Parkinson's and that research has provided insights into the cause of the disease in general. In families with Parkinson's, researchers have shown two types of genetic causes. One involves abnormalities of alpha-synuclein, a protein that accumulates in degenerating neurons in people with Parkinson's. The other involves problems with the systems in the body that dispose of unwanted proteins. It now appears that both factors play a key role in the development of Parkinson's in all people.

People with unusual exposure to herbicides and pesticides are more likely to develop Parkinson's disease than are people who don't have this exposure. Researchers haven't yet been able to connect a specific herbicide or pesticide to the disease. Several drugs taken for extended periods of time or in excessive dosages can cause symptoms of Parkinson's disease. These include medications such as haloperidol (Haldol) and chlorpromazine (Thorazine), which are prescribed for certain psychiatric disorders, as well as drugs used to treat nausea, such as metoclopramide (Reglan, Metoclopramide HCL). The epilepsy drug valproate (Depakene) also may cause some of the features of Parkinsonism, especially severe tremor. These medications do not cause Parkinson's disease, however, and symptoms disappear when the drugs are stopped. So as can be seen from the brief above this disease is not nice and believe me this was my hardest challenge to date. How was I to recover from this one, would my self-belief and inner energy guide me over this hurdle?

The tests now started to see what had caused mine and guess what, it was Idiopathic, there seemed to be no known cause. This fired up my thirst for knowledge; I read whatever I could on the disease. I started to become a prolific reader; I studied the great writers and poets, the mysteries of creation and the Universe. My thirst for knowledge was unquenchable. If I was to live with this disease then I was to put to work my mind and keep it active.

I was determined not to let this or my past defeat me. What I need is not a tensionless state but rather the striving and struggling for some goal worthy of me. What I need is not the discharge of tension at any cost, but the call of a potential meaning waiting to be fulfilled, by me. I who become conscious of the responsibility I have toward other human beings who affectionately wait for me, or to an unfinished work, I will never be able to throw away my life or let this disease defeat me.

Living With Bad Health

My Motto: *"I now know the "why" for my existence and will now be able to understand the "how."*

My meaning of life has three distinct phases –

✓ by accepting a challenge;
✓ by experiencing a gain, loss or hurt;
✓ by suffering to achieve the solution;

To learn and understand these and realise their meaning can help you overcome any hurdle or challenge. Why am I telling you all this, well to help you understand that no matter what life throws at you in challenges you can always turn a negative into a positive.

Living with any chronic illness can be difficult, and it's normal to feel angry, depressed, or discouraged at times. Parkinson's disease presents special problems because it can cause chemical changes in your brain that make you feel anxious or depressed. Furthermore, Parkinson's disease can be profoundly frustrating, especially in the advanced stages when ordinary tasks take longer to carry out and walking, talking and even eating become more difficult. Day to day tasks such as bathing, dressing become a frustrating and embarrassing chore.

The first thing I had to do was to learn all I could about my illness. Find out how the disease progresses, my prognosis, and treatment options and their side effects. The more I knew the more active I can be in my own home. In addition to talking to my health care team, I looked for and read all information and books as well as information on the Internet, including the Web sites of various Parkinson's disease organizations.

I became very pro-active, although I often felt anxious and discouraged; I could not let others including my family and doctors make important decisions for me. I had to take an active role in my treatment. Maintaining a dedicated support system, I felt was important. Strong relationships are crucial in dealing with chronic illnesses. Although friends and family are my best allies, the understanding of people who know what I am going through can be especially helpful. Support groups aren't for everyone, but for many people, they can be a useful resource for practical information about Parkinson's disease. I found that I developed lasting bonds with people who are going through the same experiences. Support groups also exist for the families of people with Parkinson's disease. I needed to approach work differently, and this proved far too difficult and disruptive. I then had to consider whether my symptoms were affecting my ability to perform each task. I needed to minimise work-related stress, this I found was too difficult and had to give work away. A diagnosis of Parkinson's disease doesn't mean every sufferer has to stop working.

Although I did not feel comfortable talking about my illness, in many cases it's best to be candid and I was with my employers. That way, they could adjust but this again was not going to work. I had no legal obligation to show my condition to my employer if I could do the job, but this proved impossible. The main thing I felt in living with PD was to keep communication with my wife. I will expand here and reveal that I re-married to a lady that I owe my whole existence to, her support and undying zest to keep me going is the main reason I feel I am still here.

I feel blessed and very humble to have such a person who has given so much of herself to me and the children and never asked for anything in return. I am now focused on being someone and achieving something in life, and this in the end will be all because of her faith and belief in me, and the love we share.

It's extremely important for couples to be open about their feelings, especially when it comes to living with Parkinson's disease. The disease changed my life and the lives of my loved ones in several ways. Here there is a big BUT, not only was it Parkinson's Disease that change my life, some years ago in 2015, I fell and injured my back and had to undergo three surgeries. The third was Fusion with plate and screws, but all went wrong and not going into detail, it gave me with a disease known as Cauda Equina Syndrome (CES), where all the nerves controlling my bladder, bowel and sexual function all disappeared. I also have permanent pins and needles in both legs and walk with a limp.

The side effects from this syndrome are ugly and just three years later had to have my bladder removed for reasons that were connected to the CES, and my kidney detached during the operation causing a stay in the Intensive Care Unit (ICU). Due this I now only have the function of one kidney, suffer Post Traumatic Stress Syndrome (PTSD), and severe Anxiety from all the events that have occurred, but I am still above ground and take each day as a new beginning, thus the revision of and writing of this edition of The Life Handbook of Challenges.

I have found it best to talk honestly about these events within my life. For you in the first instance, if you're no longer able to work full time, there may be financial issues that need to be resolved. The amount of care a person with Parkinson's disease and other problems are also often an issue. Because it may take you longer to do ordinary tasks, your partner might want to help. But most people with Parkinson's or CES like to remain as independent as possible. I needed to let my wife know when I needed help and when I didn't. We sometimes experienced a little anger as I would not always be forthcoming in telling what I needed. Parkinson's and CES makes it more difficult to move easily, which can affect day to day living. I found the most important thing, was to talk frankly about my feelings and concerns. Repressed feelings can be harmful to my immediate well-being and long-term health. It was necessary for me to discuss my problems with my psychologist.

The main thing I found the hardest was to be honest with my children. I made the mistake in the first instance trying to hide the diagnosis from them. Children can usually sense when something is wrong in the family and the anxiety and fear of not knowing is often harder on them than knowing the truth. I needed in the end to sit down with them and explain the circumstances and in addition, I needed to reassure them that their mother and father will be all right and will still be there for them. I decided then to answer my children's questions honestly to help them cope. I knew from now on that life was not going to be the same and that I could not just rely on my will and strength to get me through I needed the support.

To turn a positive into a negative is
'The seed of equivalent benefit'

'Ted Joslin'

"When we understand that man is the only animal who must create meaning, which must open a wedge into neutral nature, we already understand the essence of love. Love is the problem of an animal that must find life, create a dialogue with nature to experience his own being. I think that taking life seriously means something such as this: that whatever man does on this planet has to be done in the lived truth of the terror of creation, of the grotesque, of the rumble of panic and stress underneath everything. Otherwise, it is false. Whatever is achieved must be achieved with the full exercise of passion, of vision, of pain, of fear, and of sorrow. How do we know … that our part of the meaning of the universe might not be a rhythm in sorrow?"

'Ernest Becker'

This statement of *Ernest Becker* was the changing of my thinking and over the ensuing years I started to realise that having this disease and CES and the troubles I had, and what I was doing with my life was causing me stress and heartache, as well as upset for my family. This statement was a blessing in disguise. It created a whole new world, a whole new outlook on who and what I was, and why I was here. I started to write with fervour and before too long had almost eight manuscripts in all stages of completion. I did not want to have them published, it was an outlet an extension of my being to put into words what I felt in my poems and my imagination ran wild for the mystery thrillers, and investigative books I had penned.

Also, in 1996 a terrible event happened in my home state in Australia, and it shook me to think that my home state could be the site for such horrific and terrible loss of life. Again, a challenge was thrown up to me by instinct of humanity and wisdom. I could not rest easy with what was being told and reported about this incident so I challenged myself to author a book that would I hope be published on my investigation into this matter. I am striving to achieve this, and I will do it.

I then set myself another challenge, to write about the atrocities my ancestors suffered as convicts, again, my work I hope will be published. So, to this book and how I have found that writing and seeking out life experiences and how they have made me grow and develop, I felt it was time to tell the world, no matter what life hands you or you believe it has given you as another hurdle to either mount or succumb to, all the challenges or obstacles in life are there for a reason.

You must be open and receptive to what is being told to you and shown to you. The pain, anguish, agony of the fall they all have meaning and a message for us to adhere to and to look for and understand their meaning.

'We Have to Find Our Own Way and True Path in Life'

The First Lesson of a Challenge

Remember this is my solution for facing life and its pitfalls or challenges. I have survived the last 30 years putting the following into practice. I give it to you the reader to try.

Martin Luther King Jr, in one of his many speeches said;

"An individual has not started living until he can rise above the narrow confines of his individualistic concerns to the broader concerns of all humanity".

This is so true, we need to remember we were created to live as one and to each we are individual. We were not created to cause war or to fight with one another. We have an inherit instinct to save Humanity. Take world disasters, we all feel for those who suffer loss, but there are only certain numbers of people who instantly move to help and support those who have suffered. Why is it that each of us feel remorse or heartfelt sympathy for those who have suffered, but again there are but a few who act.

I raise this here as this is how your own mind works. You are diagnosed with a disease or a challenge in some form that is thrown upon you. Immediately your mind looks for a clue or reason for this event happening. It then looks for sympathy because of this challenge and it feels lost, alone, unwanted. Finally, there are those who will help and those who will not. I can speak from experience this happens to us all, but only a small percentage of humanity will admit it. Here is the first problem and why the world has wars and dissention. Pride and stubbornness to allow one to be aided or helped in some way denies us the ability to see the full extent of our challenge and can we only see the solution from one perspective.

Yes, this will suffice but does it completely dissolve the problem. Has the hurdle or challenge been completely and fully defeated? The answer is **NO**. Any problem, challenge or hurdle has two sides, the up and the downside. Like any story, movie, situation even life there are two sides. Within the ensuing pages I will show how I figure out the two sides of my life and how it has helped me to focus on the now and the future.

Many of us have dreams and ambitions, which we either achieve or not. Why do some achieve and fulfil their dreams, while others never seem to even get close. The reason in my opinion is self-belief and weighing up the two sides. Two very pertinent and true focuses for me now is a book known as *"The Secret"* by Rhonda Byrne. This book shows us we all have that inner strength and determination and how the universe is you and I and how we create our own universe within a universe.

This book inspired me and lifted me that one rung further to open and write down my hurdles and challenges. The other was an inspirational lecture by Dr John De Martini, a man who literally lifted himself from the gutter, overcame dyslexia and became an inspiration to all.

"A turning point is life's way of giving you a chance to move ahead spiritually, though you must reach for the gift yourself."

'Harold Klemp'

****

"I give it to you as a gift from me, know it can help in many ways, do not join the thought of struggle, but join the idea of living the best one can be."

'Feebee Newlands'

****

With what is handed to us, we receive with no questions and never seem to refuse or look for an excuse to turn our back on that gift. What we work and strive for in life we always repeatedly ask questions and find excuses why we cannot achieve our goals or dreams. Firstly, let us look at what we are striving for, and ask the following questions:

32

1. Is the Dream or Goal realistically achievable?

2. Will it help oneself in the future?

3. Why did we decide on this item or goal?

4. What steps are needed to achieve our aim?

5. By accepting a challenge, will we learn from it?

6. By experiencing a gain, loss or hurt is it worth suffering to achieve the solution?

Is The Dream or Goal Realistic and Achievable?

Only you can answer this question. Many of us try to aim far beyond our abilities and end up not only losing focus on what we want to achieve but lose our focus and determination because we have not been either honest or realistic with ourselves. I mentioned earlier about two sides to achieving something well here is an example. I hear you say, "Why then can Joe and Nora achieve this?" My answer is look at the two sides of the goal. Has Joe or Nora done anything different, have they formulated a list of steps to be taken to achieve their aim? Have you done either of these steps, what advantages has Joe or Nora got, that you do not? For anyone and I mean anyone it does not matter there has to be a logical plan to be able to achieve anything.

In life we must eat and drink to survive the other side of the story or plan as told there is two sides is, we must use the bathroom to get rid of the waste. I realise this is teaching you a simple plan and executing it but in life this is how anything works. There is always two sides to whatever you do, another example is you buy a drink; the second side is you pay and consume that item.

Here we can bring in *Isaac Newton's Laws of Motion,* i.e.: *'for all actions there is an equal and opposite reaction'* the same avails in life and whatever you do.

Thus, we come back to the heading of this section, for your dream or goal to be realistic, what is the up and down sides as well as is it achievable and what are the gains and consequences of achieving that. Nothing in life is given without some form of gain or loss, thus those two small words become the two sides of the list that will make your goal or dream achievable and realistic.

Sceptics will say; *"but love is given without gain or loss,"* I ask; *"how does one give love?"* Love is an emotion, and as I mentioned in my Introduction an emotion equates to touch. We say that he/she touched my heart with love, thus the emotion of love is shown. The gain here is that the love/emotion given has been fulfilling, the loss will be that the emotion will be but for a moment. I realise this is a simplistic look at this area but it explains how we have the two sides to everything. Another example is we shake hands with someone we meet. The emotion is touch, the gain is the feeling of welcoming and peace, and loss is that once the handshake is complete the touch/emotion is gone.

Will it help oneself in the future?

The next area we must discuss is what will be the benefits of our dream or goal. The main issue here again brings in the earlier section in making the goal achievable and realistic so that the benefits will be untold for you in the future. Although this area is important it is brief in that it ties in all the questions and the answers that one gives are the resultant benefits. But we must really be honest when looking at the benefits and the future. Will the dream or goal be the fulfilment and serve me to achieve a better life and create the future that I want?

We again look at the two sides here, remember, nothing as explained in life, the universe, or any living thing, always has two sides minimum. The benefit to us in the future must first fulfil the goal or dream we have created and to offset any downside or cost we will incur to achieve what we want. Then will the cost of this goal or dream leave us in a struggling situation in the present before we achieve the aim and the future benefits. As you see there are two sides that must be answered, and the benefits for the future must outweigh the struggles or problems created in the present.

Why did we decide on this goal or dream?

Now, this is the time of honesty to oneself and where the real lessons in Life's Challenges start. We all have desires, dreams, and unfulfilled aspects of our life. There is not one human being alive; in my opinion has everything he/she wants. You may say the King of England has everything, I doubt that does he have full freedom to walk the streets unprotected, to go to a cinema without bodyguards, No! So, the King has lost here the real freedom of life, to be able to decide and carry out an action without incurring the aid of others and basically asking permission. The same goes for any person in power or who has money. There is always an area that needs to be questioned before any of us can fully commit to our dream, or goal.

Please do not get the idea I am against having money or power, I am not, but to be able to make a free choice on what to do in life and not require consent or people watching out for me is a feeling I like. Admittedly persons in power and the rich can afford to be protected and have achieved this status whether by self-achievement or an inherited gift, they still had the choice to either take or refuse. This is where the decision on our dreams or goals comes into play. The decision we made on the item etc., will it serve us well and do we need to involve others once we have achieved what we want. To involve others is a challenge as those people have their own challenges and desires as well as their own set of values. Life's Challenges are never easy and never involve just one single entity. We must use knowledge and intuition to gain, we did not get these two assets free. They were given by someone else, teaching us to use our intuition and the knowledge came from reading as well as our schooling and self-learning. Thus, we have already in reaching the stage we are presently at used others to gain something, and yes, we have had a loss to effect that. The Loss we feel, being our freedom as we gained knowledge; and the loss of time in learning how to use our intuition. Thus, when we decide on our goal, dream, or an item we wish for we must make sure that our decision will be true and honest and cause no-one else any loss.

Thus, my first real Life Challenge solution comes in here:

"Do we love ourselves enough to sacrifice something to gain what we want without hurt to the world around us?"

What steps are needed to achieve our aim?

This may seem an irrelevant question considering the earlier paragraphs, and some might say it should be a question asked sooner in our steps to achieve our aim. Well, we cannot formulate the steps to achieving something unless we know what it is we want, what it will cost, what are the benefits, and what are the consequences?

Thus, we now must set out our list of steps as to how we can go ahead with our goal to gain what we want. This section is like a flight of stairs, each step must be strong, have a purpose and above all lead somewhere. To have a staircase that has no rigidity is always going to be suspect and whenever we use it, we always have that sense of the stairs giving way, being unsafe. The purpose for them is to go up or down as the case may be and they always lead to an area we wish to enter. Thus, our steps to gain our desires must be strong; they cannot give way to outside influences and cause us to stray from the path of our dreams. If the steps are not strong then this will cause our whole plan to gain our goal to collapse and be influenced by others who may not be sincere in helping us or are unable to create their own steps and goals and wish to either steal ours or cause disruption to us gaining our dream.

"Your steps must lead somewhere and

show a result"

The steps must also have purpose, in being useful, so that as we ascend each one toward our goal or dream, it is an achievement and a fulfilment of one part of that which we want. When you go upstairs within your house or steps when walking, each step taken raises you closer to the upper floor in the house or you gain the position you wish to be at.

Say that every second step was missing, you will still gain the result but you will work harder for it. It is the same in setting the steps for your dreams or goals, do not skip steps, as it will not only cost you time in achieving that for which you wish but also be unsafe as the strength will not be there. Finally, the steps you set down must lead to that which you want. They must be achievable, have direction that takes you on the quickest but safest path and above all they have a minimal cost to you personally and will not interfere or cause others disruption in their move through life. This last area must be the most important when setting your steps. To cause others disruption and use them for your own gain is achieving nothing.

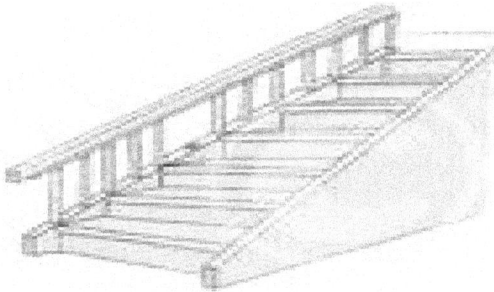

"One Step at a time will get you there safely"

Your goal or dream is yours and therefore you and you alone can achieve the fulfilment and feel the desire of that achievement and be satisfied you did it. There is nothing to say you cannot ask for help, but providing that help does not cause the helper problems or diminish your goal or dream achievement, or even make it that you may have gained it under false pretences.

Here is my second Life Challenge solution:

"To achieve your goal is an accomplishment, gratifying, and shows you have achieved your dreams, to help others achieve their dreams is a bonus"

By accepting a challenge, will we learn from it?

When we set out to achieve a dream or goal, and we have our steps in place to follow, we also set challenges within those steps for us to gain knowledge and understanding. We cannot set a goal or dream without challenges, whether it is to buy a new car or boat, the challenge to obtain the money for the purchase. A dream is to win a lottery, the challenge to buy the ticket and hope for luck to intervene. No matter what we aim for we accept some form of challenge along the way. As said, we need steps to reach that goal, those steps no matter how many each are an individual challenge to us. We must ascend each step, thus a challenge, we must complete the tasks on each step to advance, thus a challenge. Every challenge we have had in our lives to date and those we will face in the future we will learn from.

A wise man once said, *"We learn from our mistakes"* is so true. Our mistakes were challenges we failed at, we learnt from making those errors and when the time was right and we had to perform the challenge again we completed it correctly thus advanced another step-in life.

41

Now older and as some would say wiser, we still make mistakes, thus still facing challenges, but are we learning from them? If we were all learning from our mistakes, we would have no war, no racial prejudice, no criminals, there would be a peace not previously known in our lifetime.

So, what does this tell us, that our leaders and those in power have not put strong, reliable steps in place for their plans and the steps have led them no-where and outside influences have been allowed to interfere thus they have not learnt from their mistakes. The same goes for our lives. The lesson here that I am trying to help you understand is that we must learn and correct mistakes from our everyday challenges. Every day of our existence we are faced with a challenge of one form or another.

Some of us just ignore that challenge and hope someone else will do it, or we say the problem is not ours, or we face it front on and solve the challenge, whether it is alone or with help. No matter what the answer, we cannot ignore it forever as some of those problems or challenges will one day come back to haunt us, and may cause us either grief, hurt or loss. Face the challenge and all its variables; be prepared for what the outcome maybe. Never turn your back as they do not go away, they just drift around and return when we least expect.

Here is my Third Life Challenge solution:

"Turn a challenge into a positive, and then put steps in place to overcome the challenge, learn from the outcome and use it for the future."

By experiencing a gain, loss or hurt is it worth suffering to achieve the solution?

Now, the real grit of this chapter as we have shown, you need to plan for your goal, understand the benefits, the reasons behind your decision, and the steps to achieve it. But, in all things to gain something there will be hurt, loss, or suffering, and the question is, are you willing to experience that to gain your goal? Please be aware by hurt etc., we do not mean that someone or something is going to take you for ten rounds of the kitchen and hurt you physically; the hurt we express here is mental hurt and suffering. In all avenues of life where we are to gain or learn something we have along the road suffered a hurt or suffering mentally. Take for example your school days, you were asked a question; you got it wrong, your classmates laughed at you and the teacher scowled.

Mentally, you were hurt by embarrassment in not knowing the answer when you should have and you suffered mentally because of this.

It has happened to us all at some time or other; no-one is alone in this area. It also happens in everyday adult life and this is the challenges we face. Challenges of our lives each day a wide and varied, they are large and small, easy or difficult, but no matter what they are a challenge; some would also call them a test. We face almost eighty percent of these challenges daily without realising that they are a challenge, e.g.: getting out of bed, eating breakfast, going to work or school, driving a motor vehicle, all challenges that we do by instinct and from knowledge and intuition that we have gotten during our lifetime to date. We do these as a natural course, but have you ever stopped and thought what the benefits are, what are the steps, what will I gain etc. No, we never ask those questions because we have been trained to do them as a natural progression in Life, they are a *HABIT*.

A habit, the dictionary explains this is a continuous act done on a repetitious basis. Well, why is it we cannot set ourselves goals and dreams and make them a habit. We can, and this will be discussed in the next chapter, because before we can form a habit we need to know how to cope with the loss or suffering and the gain of changing our present thinking and habits on challenges. As said, to achieve something there must be a loss and a gain, the two sides of the question again come into play. When you have made your decision and have all in place for your goal or your dream, there must be a loss and gain list, this is like an addendum to your steps. This list tells you what will be lost as you take each step and what taking that step will gain you. Thus, as you advance towards your goal, your losses and hurt should be offset by the gains and be of equal number, if not then if there are too many losses then is the dream or goal achievable and are the benefits worth the result.

If the gains outweigh the losses, then you must make sure that the benefits of your goal or dream will be there in the future and are they sustainable. Rest assured *EVERYONE* experiences these challenges in their lives! It can leave you feeling powerless and overwhelmed. Your ability to cope with these challenging situations directly decides your level of well-being. Yet, as you progress through life, you rarely can obtain the resources needed to deal with these circumstances effectively and appropriately.

This book aims to give you the skills to hold those moments and build on them, using the two sides and bring them together as one. When we achieve that we will be able to gain what we want and keep our dreams. Sometimes our goals and dreams may disrupt others as one lifts themselves from where they were to where they know their focus lies. Keep your focus and those who feel the disruption may even support you on your journey.

Never be someone else's puppet, be *YOURSELF*!!!

Frightened if you try something new it will blow up in your face !!!

Habits

A habit is something you can do without thinking which is why most of us have so many of them.

'Frank A. Clark'

****

We have briefly touched on what a habit is, but why do we have them and how do they affect our mind, body and spirit in our everyday living? Sorry to bring in a bit of medical ability here to help explain why we create a habit but I believe if we know the how and why, we will be able to understand our habits better. There is a scientific reason and have you ever arrived at home or work with no memory of how you got there? When you started on your journey, you thought about the first few steps on that familiar path, but somewhere along the way, your brain moved onto more interesting topics, and the next thing you knew, you'd arrived. This is the essence of habits, once you start on a familiar series of actions, you stop thinking about them, and you can complete them without conscious thought or attention. This can be both a boon and a bane to humans as it frees up our minds from dull or repetitive tasks, but also makes it difficult to stop a habit once it's started.

- What differentiates the learning that forms habits from other types of learning?

- How do habits form?

- Why are habits so hard to break?

- How does the brain know which learned behaviours to translate into habits?

- What does this imply about our day-to-day behaviour?

Habits are a series of steps learned gradually and sometimes without conscious awareness. Habit formation is a type of procedural learning in which the basal ganglia, a cluster of nuclei found in the forebrain between the cortex and the brainstem, play a key role. The location of the basal ganglia provides access to both the cognitive areas of the brain involved in decision making (forebrain) and the midbrain which controls motor movement.

It is the only place in the brain that deals with both physical and cognitive actions simultaneously, linking thought to movement. This linking occurs via projections from the basal ganglia into the thalamic nuclei (associated with the frontal cortex and cognitive functions) and the brainstem nuclei (associated with motor control). The area of the basal ganglia that has been particularly associated with habit formation is called the striatum. This area receives the most input from the cortex and may be involved in cortico-basal ganglia loops using the thalamic connections mentioned above. These loops may be involved in the decision to select certain actions, e.g. the automatised response of habits. In addition, the striatum receives input from dopamine-containing neurons in the midbrain or brainstem. Together, these inputs may create a loop with the striatum that leads to habit formation by associating rewards (dopamine) with a particular context.

Although the exact mechanism is still unknown at this point, the coding of tasks into units or chunks is supported by behaviours like obsessive-compulsive disorder (OCD). The striatum of OCD patients shows consistent abnormal patterns of activity that abate with treatment. The symptoms of OCD involve sequential repetitive behaviours driven by extraordinary compulsions. These behaviours are performed as chunks and are linked to the striatum by the patterns of activity mentioned above. Chunking of tasks allows for the automated nature of habit behaviour. In fact, attention to the tasks involved in a habit could lead to its disruption.

This emphasizes the importance of slow learning in habits. This gradual development offers a selection mechanism for which task sequences will be encoded as habits. Only those tasks which are repeated over a period have the potential to become habits. This is particularly important since the predictive firing of dopamine-containing neurons and the chunking of habit steps makes it especially difficult to break a habit once it is formed.

Since a habit is a series of behaviours bound together and started by a particular context, avoiding this initiating step could be key to breaking a habit. Habits are formed by the repetition of a particular neural pathway leading to a reward. When a habit is being formed, learning creates a bombardment of action potentials that strongly depolarize a target cell so that fewer action potentials are needed to trigger depolarization in the future. This can create a neural pathway, a series of connected neurons whose polarization is permanently raised closer to the threshold potential making it easier to propagate action potentials down this path. To break a habit, it might be necessary to prevent neural pathways from being selected. This could be done by creating new neural pathways that are preferred, i.e. making a new habit to take the place of the undesirable one.

The importance of the initiating step in performance of habits is underscored by certain behaviours associated with Parkinson's (here comes the reason for this book). Since the release of dopamine is associated with the beginning step of a habit, a lack of predictive ability, i.e. the ability to predict a reward and release dopamine at the start of a habit chunk, could impair sensor motor functionality. This would lead to behaviours like those displayed by Parkinson's patients, in which they have difficulty starting and stopping movement sequences, or switching from one sequence to another, thus making it extremely difficult for a PD sufferer to break a habit or start a new one. The role of the basal ganglia in task switching is illustrated by a decrease in this ability by patients with basal ganglia damage. For example, patients with Huntington's disease made significantly more errors in selecting a sample item from a group of items which were identical to the sample along one dimension. This shows a difficulty in switching attention between dimensions, thus linking the basal ganglia with the ability to readily switch between learned procedures or habits.

The acquisition and performance of habits can also be manipulated by certain drugs. It is in fact this manipulation of the habit formation process that could be the underlying mechanism of addiction. For example, there is heightened activity in the striatum which is associated with a proportionate increase in stereotyped behaviour when people use drugs such as cocaine or amphetamine. This heightened activity may act like a switch in the basal ganglia which changes a habit into an addiction.

Since even one dose of these drugs can be addictive, the gradual, repetitive nature of habit formation is started, possibly due to a chemical change from the sudden, massive reward of a high. Thus, to change this habit the user needs to break the cycle. The idea of the basal ganglia as a key player in habit formation is further strengthened by studies which dissociate other areas of the brain associated with learning and memory, e.g. the hippocampus and the amygdala, from habit formation. The hippocampus is involved in explicit, factual learning and memories.

The amygdala supports emotional memory. Habits are differentiated from other types of learning both structurally (basal ganglia changes) and behaviourally (incrementally, unconsciously bought). They are essentially discrete, quantized patterns of behaviour that make up major portions of individual everyday existence. The complexity of conscious behaviours requires the surrender of routine tasks to the unconscious to allow a basic level of multi-tasking. For example, habits allow us to walk around the block and talk to companion at the same time, to eat while we watch TV, to find our way home while dissecting the exam we just took in our mind. While this is certainly convenient in many ways, this surrender of control also leads to questions about free will.

Can habits alter one's brain structure in such a way that free will is lost? Isn't this the essence of addictions? How is the conflict between one's conscious will and the unconscious force of habits reconciled? I hope this has not bored you, but it leads into the forming of new habits.

*A **'Bad Habit'** is a continuous exercise that can*

be monotonous and achieves nothing.

Remember it only takes 30 days to form a habit but 120 days to break it.

The Habit Cycle

TRIGGER: Someone yells at you, or something goes wrong. Triggers can come from our environment or inside ourselves.

ACTION: You drink, smoke, or overeat. Actions can be taken towards us or others.

NEED: Being human means having needs. A basic human need is to feel understood.

THOUGHTS: When we deny or repress our needs, we retreat into a world of thoughts. This can be filled with criticisms, judgments, blame, and confusion.

EMOTIONS: The emotions that arise are often decided by the thoughts that preceded it. We often avoid feeling emotions by numbing them or acting them out.

IMPULSE: When we resist or control our true needs and their thoughts and feelings, we create pressure in our system that urgently seeks relief. The relief-seeking impulse is often a misguided attempt to get the original need met.

THOUGHTS: Judgmental thoughts continue to arise about our inner experience.

ACTION: An action happens to alleviate the pressure and meet the need. This is only a short-term pleasure. In our haste, the action is often not the one that meets our true need.

THOUGHTS: Judgments about our habits become the new **Trigger** and the cycle begins again.

Enduring habits I hate.... Yes, at the very bottom of my soul I feel grateful to all my misery and bouts of sickness and everything about me that is imperfect, because this sort of thing leaves me with a hundred backdoors through which I can escape from enduring habits.
'*Friedrich Nietzsche*'

****

It is true that we have the desire to stop doing the thing that we perceive as being bad. But the reason we normally cannot break the habit, and the real problem is, we have another desire that is even greater than our desire to break the bad habit.

That is our desire to continue to do it. And the reason we normally want to continue to do it is because it brings enjoyment or pleasure of some kind. We would not do it if we did not like it. Some habits like drinking are formed as a means of escaping from the pains of reality. Other habits like overeating may bring us a sense of false satisfaction or momentary relief from stress. Some habits like smoking even bring us substitute feelings of pleasure to replace the ones we really want but cannot have. Many habits are combined with other habit like temper and swearing. We cannot control our temper so we swear to try to vent the feelings of the anger. The habits we have do not come by some accident. Each one has its purpose in our lives. That is why we start these habits in the first place.

As we resolve to stop these *"BAD"* habits, we find ourselves caught in a war of emotions between the two desires, and the stronger of the two desires within us will always win out. When we resolve to quit, then fall back into the habit, all we have done is just let the desire to do, overpower the desire to not do.

"Conditioning" a learned behaviour.

It has a great bearing on human behaviour especially as it relates to habits. We are all very prone to develop a habit that is done at a certain time and a certain place. Then when we enter that place, we feel the urge to do that thing even if we don't really want to. Ask any smoker and they will tell you about that. If they smoke every time they stop at a red light while driving the car, try to get them to come to a red light and not light up. The urge is triggered by the light not the need for the smoking.

Conditioning is a powerful thing. And it is normally associated with a time and a place. Any good student will tell you that they study at the same time and in the same place every day, and they never study in their bedroom. They have conditioned themselves to sleep when they go into the bedroom. So, if they study there too, especially on the bed, they start to send mixed signals to their body and find they cannot do either very well in the bed. That is conditioning.

When we have a habit, especially a very addictive habit that seems almost impossible to break, we will notice that we normally are taken into the performance of that habit in the same "conditions" every time, and normally under the same circumstances. So, if we honestly want to break the habit, we will almost certainly have to change our habit by not putting ourselves in that circumstance anymore. If you want to stop swearing you first must stop losing your temper for example.

\This is no easy thing to do. But again, if we take an alcoholic example, if a person has been addicted to drinking, and they always drank in some certain bar, it would be dangerous for them to go to that very same bar again and sit at the same stool and just smell the froth of the beer. If you honestly want to quit a habit, you must change the conditioning. When you go into that circumstance, it sets off a trigger inside you. The psychological triggering in your brain can be much stronger than the reality psychological trigger.

You can be trained to be hungry by a bell more than by hunger from not eating for a long time. In fact, if you go without eating for a couple of days you stop being hungry. We must remove the triggers from our lives. Discover where it is that you do what you do that is the habit. Watch for what sets you off and causes that pulling feeling or desire to do it. Then start to avoid it. Triggers can be subtle things. If you keep going back to the same circumstances and letting the triggers, be set off, you have little hope of quitting the habit. You will feel the emptiness, then the numbness than the hopelessness and finally totally lose the desire to quit and change.

Reticular Activation

The principle is that you put a rubber band on your wrist and then when you think a bad thought, or you are tempted to do whatever it is that you want to stop doing in other words your habit, you give that little rubber band a flip. The negative feedback is not overwhelming but your mind will start to lean to avoid the thought or action you want to quit to avoid the pain on the wrist. It is a highly effective tool. Try it. Very few people ever fell into an addictive habit by a blow-out. Almost no one became a smoker overnight. Very few people are immoral on the first date. It normally comes by a series of slow leaks. One step builds on another. There never is a day when you can say that is enough. I am hooked. I must quit.

It is easy to say, why don't you just stop eating to an overweight person. Have you ever tried it? It is easy to say how you can smoke when you know that it will kill you. Have you ever tried to stop smoking? Before you point a finger, let him that is without sin cast the first stone. May we all look at the beam in our own eye before trying to remove the mote from our brothers' eye? Every weakness has its cause. Every person chained to a habit has a reason, not an excuse, why they were entrapped. Our best hope is to help them not to criticize them. Thus, this book is helping you not to criticise.

One of the reasons that we keep doing what it is that we are doing is because we get so frustrated that you stop caring and give up so when you are frustrated you don't care and give in anyway. We get so discouraged that we don't care so when we are discouraged, we do it again. We give in and smoke or eat or become lazy and lethargic anyway. We get so angry that we don't care so when we lose our temper we swear anyway.

We get so depressed that we don't care so when we are depressed, we do it anyway. The feelings from the touch and burn after we have done it again are not sufficiently painful to make us resist before we give in. We must find a way to care. We do it so we don't have the bad empty feeling after. That is hard sometimes to remember the bad that comes after when we want the pleasure we perceive before. Looking across the bridge to the other side of the act is a great key in helping us quit if we can do it? I often think of what Anthony Robins said about losing weight. He said, *"Nothing tastes so good as thin feels"*. I think that can be applied to any habit breaking if we find the goal of what we want more than having what we get from the pleasure or relief of frustration from the bad habit.

You are the one that you must report back to in the end. It is you who will suffer for the pain of unpleasant habits if you get them. It is you, as well, who will enjoy the blessings of a pure life and the opening of the windows of dreams and goals if you do not get unhealthy habits. There are rewards that come from control that cannot be had if you are out of control.

"The choice is yours."

Not sure if your family and friends will like the

NEW YOU ?

Remember Fear knocked at the door. Faith
answered.

No one was there!!!

Self-Confidence

Self-confidence is a belief in yourself and what you want in life, based on an implicit trust in your own abilities to deal with the things that come your way in life. You will find that with greater self-confidence, you will have a more positive mindset and greater faith in your actions and choices, despite what others may have to say about you. Self-confidence can be developed, so fret not if you find that you are lacking in it. With some practice and the following 5 steps, you will find yourself building up your self-confidence!

Step One: Find your own issues and own them!

I tell people that the challenges said are my own personal issues and that everyone must find their own. Think about your strengths and how you can play to them, as well as your weaknesses and how you can improve upon them. Do not let your ego get in the way of over inflating your strengths, nor in downplaying your weaknesses.

Step Two: Avoid all negative statements about you!

The comments that you make about yourself, or to yourself, has a significant impact on your self-confidence. If you are thinking negative thoughts, it will lead to negative feelings about your situation and yourself. You may not realize it, but negative or self-deprecating comments over time will erode your self-confidence.

Step Three: Believe in yourself and your abilities!

Beliefs are things that we know to be true and accept as true without needing to question or consider it. Believe that you can do what someone else can do, and you will be able to achieve it as well. To achieve such a level of self-confidence for the earlier statement to be true, you must first start believing in yourself to empower it. Hence, controlling what you believe is the key towards creating a life that you want. The key to building self-confidence is to believe in you.

If you have trouble trying out something new, it is not a terrible thing to initially stick with what you're familiar with. This will help you feel more confident and give you the assurance to go ahead onto something new. By going into something new with a cheerful outlook and belief in your abilities, you will find it easier to be confident and act confident. Over time, you will find that your comfort zone will have increased significantly, as will your self-confidence.

Step Four: Self Affirmation, looking in the mirror!

Just as it is important to avoid negative thoughts; positive thoughts are encouraged and have an uplifting effect on your emotions and confidence. Make a list of your accomplishments, no matter its size, and acknowledge them. The power of the mind cannot be underestimated. If you want something strongly enough, let it be the motivating force.

Step 5: Perseverance

There will always be setbacks in life, and we must learn to be more resilient to bounce back from these. When things do not go the way you planned, it is alright to be tough with yourself if you were to blame. The crux is not in just taking or laying the blame, but in figuring out what went wrong and how you can fix it. If the problem is something outside the scope of your control, it was not your fault in the first place.

Do not let the downs in life get to you.

Take the time to think through what happened, and how you can avoid it from happening again. If you feel that you need a confidence boost, speak to your friends and your family to put things in perspective.

Take the time to put these 5 simple steps into practice, and you will be well on your way to building up your self-confidence. Meet your problems head on and learn how to deal with different situations. It is alright to be afraid, or to fail, the key is to keep moving forward and working on improving your self-confidence.

Further to Self Confidence is Attitude*:*

- We all react differently to change.

- Some readily adapt.

- Some ignore it and hope that life will return to the status quo.

- Others actively seek it out.

As a person, your success, or failure, depends in part on how well you adapt to change. What your attitude is going to be. Do you run screaming like a banshee towards it, ready to conquer? Or do you go sit in a closet, close your eyes, and wait and hope for it to go away, hoping that everything will return to "normal"?

The most successful entrepreneurs not only embrace change, but they also actively seek it out knowing that greater fulfilment, greater success, and greater profits come with constant adaptation to the market. My personal experience has led me to reengineer my life so far with fabulous results; as I start down one path, things have happened that open my eyes to another path—one I may not have been ready or able to see previously. My life is ever evolving and I wouldn't have it any other way. To wish for change means a change of Attitude, to reach a dream or goal requires a change of habits and attitude.

How about you?

Are you a #1:
Actively searching for things to change to engineer a perfect life. Do you run about shaking trees to see what will fall out and how you can use that information to your advantage?

Or #2
You don't particularly love change but knows to look for the opportunities that abound whenever it occurs. In the world, are you the man/woman who rises to manager almost overnight and no one knows how or why this happened (you saw an opportunity and JUMPED on it). In the entrepreneurial world, you sell dry wood and hot meals from a cart you pull through the campground on an unexpected rainy day. You look at any change and find the opportunity that lies within.

Or Are You a #3
Every time change rears its head, you can be found hiding and wishing that everything would stay as it was and that you don't need to learn new skills or improve old ones. You are usually blaming someone, anyone, else for the change to justify hiding. In your world, change is something to be feared. You can often be found working in the same job, in the same company until you are forced out.

Most of us tend to fall into either the "2" or "3" personality mode with the occasional "1" appearance. Change is not going away - if anything, the rate at which it happens is exponentially increasing - especially with the internet. To succeed, you must be able to predict, deal with and adapt to change and the sooner, the better. This is a new habit with attitude. One of the most important things is to look at the situation objectively and understand that you have control over your thoughts and how you react to the change. How you think about the change will decide whether you are a "1" or a "2". *It's your life - take control!*

Positive Attitude – What Is It?

It starts with being content and self-assured with the person that you are. A strong self-image radiates love and spirit and the people who are in your company begin to feel an equivalent way. Having a positive demeanour is a pivotal feature for realizing success in all aspects of your life. Your disposition destines how you approach your life and is reflected in your occupation, business ventures, sporting efforts and relationships.

A winner's attitude is essential for achieving your desires in life. People that we applaud for achieving excellence would not have carried out their dreams by living their life with a detached disposition. The predominant ingredients for a victorious life are accepting yourself, being able to visualize your success and living with the right attitude.

A positive attitude produces a buoyant outlook on life. You will feel happier, healthier, and more energetic. Your belief in yourself and your talents will be amplified and by taking on an open and positive attitude your mind will be welcoming to the opportunities that will start to come your way. People with a negative attitude often become entirely immersed with their problems and are unable to see the opportunities that are presented to them. Once you teach your mind to automatically undertake a positive attitude your difficulties will not be as significant and you will have the ability to cope with them effortlessly.
Impulsively we are drawn towards the company of positive people. They could lift our spirits and make us feel good about life. Attitude, whether it's positive of negative, is extremely infectious - choose wisely and spend your time with positive uplifting people and your essence will imitate the same vibration.

When you choose to live your life with a positive attitude your spirit will be encircled with a light energy which will magnetically draw people towards you. Accomplishing your desires is entirely within your power, however, you must embark on life with a positive attitude and believe that whatever you desire can, and will, be achieved - connect this with a positive attitude and you will be irrepressible.

In 1903 a renowned New York engineering professor had said that it would be impossible for man to fly. Two weeks later the Wright Brothers flew the world's first powered airplane. These guys had a definite advantage - they unquestionably believed that their dream was achievable!

Don't let fear of failure hold you back from pursuing your dreams - instead, espouse a positive attitude and reach for your goals with faith. We can all learn from the Wright Brothers - anything is possible if you approach your dreams with a positive attitude and believe.

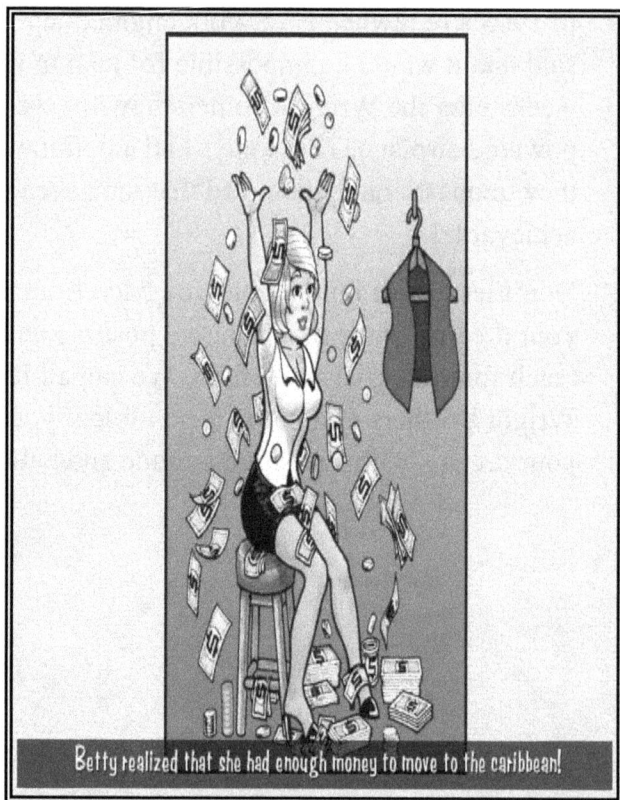

Betty realized that she had enough money to move to the caribbean!

Did Betty follow her dream with a positive attitude?

"Be whoever **YOU** want to be."

Personal Power & Motivation

All of us would love to have personal power – the power to realise our dreams, the power to be calm and forgiving in the face of fear, the power to stay centred in ourselves in the face of attack. Our society often confuses personal power - "power within" - with "power over," which is about controlling others. There is a vast difference between personal power and control. Personal power comes from an inner sense of security, from knowing who you are in your soul, from having defined your own intrinsic worth. It is the power that flows through you when you are connected to and feel your oneness with a spiritual source of guidance. It is the power that is the eventual result of doing deep inner emotional and spiritual work to heal the fears and false beliefs got in childhood. Without this inner work to heal the beliefs that create our limitations, we are stuck in our egos, our wounded selves.

The very basis of the ego is the desire for control, for power over others and outcomes. Our ego is the self we created to try to have control over getting love, avoiding pain, and feeling safe. We created our ego self in our attempt to protect ourselves from the losses we fear loss of self, loss of other, loss of security, loss of face. As children, when we didn't get the love we needed, we decided that our true Self must be unlovable. In our attempt to feel safe, we buried our true Self and created the false self – the ego, our wounded self. The ego self then went about learning how to feel safe through trying to control others and outcomes. The ego believes that having control over how people see us and feel about us, as well as over the outcome of things, will give us the safety we look for. Even if you do manage to have some control through anger, criticism, judgment, or money, this will never give you personal power. This will never fill you with peace and joy and an inner sense of safety. Control may give you a momentary sense of safety, but it will never give you the deep sense of safety that comes from knowing your intrinsic worth, the worth of your soul. If your safety and worth are being defined by externals which can be temporary your money, your looks, your performance, and your power over others you will feel anxious. We feel anxious when we attach our worth and happiness to temporal things rather than to eternal qualities, such as caring, compassion, and kindness.

For example, Mr **X** is a man who has tremendous power over others but no personal power. He has made zillions as the owner of his own company. He has a lovely wife, three grown children, and two beautiful homes. Yet **X** is often anxious. He worries about losing his money. He is easily triggered into anger when things don't go his way and people don't behave in the way he wants. Because his heart is not open, he is a very lonely and unhappy man.

He works totally out of his ego self, believing that having control through anger and money will bring him the happiness and safety he looks for. Yet he has achieved everything he believed would bring him happiness and safety and what he feels most of the time is anxious and lonely. X is empty inside. He has no sense of his true Self, no sense of the beauty within him, no sense of his lovability and intrinsic worth. His life is based on externals rather than on the spiritual values of love, compassion, honesty, and kindness. Personal power comes from embracing spiritual values rather than just earthly values. It comes from love, kindness, and compassion – toward oneself and others, more important than power over others. It comes from doing the inner work necessary to allow the soul to have dominion over the body, rather than allowing the animal instincts of fight or flight the instincts of the body to have dominion over our choices.

When the soul has dominion over the body, you have the power to manifest your dreams, to stay centred in the face of attack, to remain loving in the face of fear. When the soul has dominion over the body, you have tremendous personal power. If you are not as productive as you'd like or tend to procrastinate, you can become motivated by changing your personal style.

The trick lies in making the activities you put off more interesting, easier, and less unpleasant. One way to make a job easier is to break it into smaller jobs. If your task is to file your income tax return, you may view it as time consuming and tedious. But if you break it into smaller categories such as gather records, download tax software, and prepare a rough draft, the tasks don't seem as difficult and you are likely to complete them in considerably less time.

Some other ways to make those undesirable jobs seem more bearable are to prioritize, use self-discipline, and reward you for small accomplishments. Try to do the least desirable tasks early in the day so you'll look forward to having the rest of the day to concentrate on more pleasant jobs. Keep in mind that self-discipline is something you do for yourself, not to punish yourself.

Make a schedule and stick to it. Don't forget to reward yourself for each step you take in overcoming procrastination. Positive reinforcement goes a long way in changing negative behaviours.

Here are eight great suggestions as to how you can get motivated:

1. Tasks will seem less daunting if you break them into several steps over a few days or weeks. Don't expect yourself to do everything all at once.

2. Don't worry about doing the job perfectly. Once you quit procrastinating, you'll have more time to go back and perfect each task. Allowing yourself adequate time to finish a task will give you more time for corrections later.

3. Find a supportive co-worker or friend to help motivate you to get moving. Two minds really are better than one.

4. Don't schedule important tasks at a time of day when your energy is low. Put the most difficult tasks at the top of your list and work from there.

5. Reward yourself for reaching critical points in your least favourite jobs. Having something to look forward to is a great motivator.

6. All times of day are not equal. Reserve your most demanding activities for the time when your energy is at its highest. Save the small jobs that require little thought for the time of day when you are at your lowest productivity level. Accomplish your tasks efficiently and you will see an improvement in your time management and motivational skills.

7. Start yourself down the road to success by setting clear, attainable goals. Break tasks into smaller pieces so they will seem less difficult. Get organized and prioritize your activities from most important to least important. Ending the harder tasks will leave you feeling good about your work and motivate you to continue.

8. Keep focused on the result instead of concentrating on how hard it will be to break your old habits. Having a light at the end of the tunnel will make your efforts seem worthwhile and the reward waiting for you will keep you motivated to achieve your goals. Procrastination is unproductive and can even be harmful to your well-being if allowed to get out of control. Stop making excuses, organize your thoughts and tasks, and be on your way to get your life under control and get motivated!

Too many of us live like goldfish, swimming in the same orbit day in and day out feeling uninspired, tired, bored, and sometimes worse. Life is much too precious to waste that way. Every person has a unique purpose in life. I implore you not to waste your days berating yourself for what you don't know and don't do well. Instead, discover your strengths, passions, purpose and build your life on those.

These will help you begin the exciting journey of self-discovery.

1. We are all here for a purpose. Your being here makes a difference. Your purpose may be obscure to you and a challenge to discover. Start now. There are many resources, coaches, and books to help you with this endeavour.

2. The secret to fulfilment is self-knowledge. Start the exciting journey of discovery.

3. The second part of the secret to fulfilment is to apply your self-knowledge to what you do and how you live. The more you know, the more you can actively pursue your true purpose.

4. Don't waste time lamenting what you don't do well. Concentrate on your strengths. Those reflect who you are. Leave the other things to people who do them well.

5. Build on your strengths. Do more of them and give yourself recognition for doing the things you do well.

6. Pay attention to the minute details that you enjoy in your everyday life. Do more of them.

7. Pay attention to the intricate details you don't enjoy. Find ways to eliminate as many of them as possible.

8. Keep a journal and put particular emphasis on the things about yourself and events in your life for which you are grateful.

9. Try to release the negative aspects of your past. Try not to be imprisoned by your past. Do not define yourself by your past.

10. Jumpstart your self-esteem by giving back to the community. Volunteer in a meaningful way that suits who you are and your interests.

You will get to know and like yourself in a whole new way. Work with a friend, hire a coach, and use the resources out there, to help you with objectivity. Have someone point out the good things about you that you tend to overlook. As soon as you stop doing what you hate and start doing what you love, you may find your life more meaningful and fulfilling.

Personally motivate yourself, do not let anyone tell you how to do it.

"YOU have the *POWER!"*

Goals

You don't have to be a fantastic hero to do certain things to compete. You can be just an ordinary chap, sufficiently motivated to reach challenging goals.

'Sir Edmund Hillary'

Goals – we have a love-hate relationship with goals. We love them because they are such a great idea and are a superb way to motivate us to achieve and then to evaluate our progress; but we hate them, because for much of the time, they go Unattained and simply frustrate us. This isn't what goals should do!

I would like to suggest some straightforward and practical techniques on how you can set goals you can achieve! After all, what good is a goal if it isn't something you can achieve?

✓ You must want it!

Firstly - do not bother to set goals for things you don't really want. For example: if your partner says they want you to quit smoking or lose weight but you do not want to, why even bother setting this as a goal. If your goal(s) are not something you personally want to carry out, and they are not relevant to you, you are unlikely to succeed – because deep down you don't really want to. State your goals in a positive way – a goal should always be something you want to have, or change. Not things you or someone else think you should. Always ask yourself on a scale of 1 to 10, with 10 being totally committed and 1 being zero commitment. How committed are you to reaching your goal? If it is less than 8, you might want to reconsider the goal.

✓ Focus

Start small. Pick two or three areas that you want to work on. Too many people say to themselves, "I want to do this, and this, and this, and this," and they end up achieving nothing! Most of what you do throughout your day can be done without a lot of mental effort, but change isn't one of them. So, try to keep your focus down to a couple of things. This way you can get success in your identified areas. Here are some aspects of your life you might like to think about: Physical, Intellectual, Emotional, Spiritual, Financial, and Relationships. Now, which is the first thing on your list? The others can follow later, but for now, you should focus on two or three, no more.

✓ Goals - the long and the short

So, do you want to lose 50 pounds? Good. Long-term you will. But for now, think short-term. Don't think about losing 50 pounds by February. Think about losing 10 pounds by October 1st. This does two things. First, it makes it pressing and urgent. Instead of saying, "I still have 6 months to lose the 50 pounds" (6 months quickly disappears into 2 months, into one month – with the 50 pounds still securely in place!) your first goal is only a few weeks away, so you must get started. This is far more successful in terms of reaching your goal. Secondly, as you reach these smaller goals (your mini milestones!), you achieve a success, which gives you regular motivation and encouragement to keep going.

✓ Make it Manageable

Instead of saying, "I am going to quit my 20 smoking a day habit straight off" change this to: "I am going to smoke no more than 15 a day for a week, then 10 the next week and so on." Give yourself small victories a little at a time. It is far easier to carry out many smaller goals that make up a large goal – rather than trying for the large goal straight off!

✓ **Reward yourself along the way**

When you lose the 10 pounds by October 1st, go and order yourself large mocha with cream from 'Starbucks' (just the one though!), then get back to your goal for November 1st. This puts a little fun back into the process of self-control and self-discipline. You will look forward to and enjoy the reward and when the going gets tough, you will say things like, "two weeks to go, and only two more pounds to lose" etc – I can do it, then I can enjoy my mocha guilt free!

✓ **Be specific with your timeline**

Don't just say, "I am going to lose 10 pounds." Say, "I am going to lose 10 pounds by December 1st." This way, when you start being tempted into Belgian Chocolates in the middle of November - under the guise of buying early Christmas presents for other people, you can say, "No way, only 5 more pounds to go in three weeks and I am not going to blow it now."

✓ **Post it where you can see it**

Always keep your goal in the front of your mind. Instead of allowing yourself to 'forget' that you are trying to lose weight by ordering a big slice of cheesecake, your visual reminder will help you to choose something a little on the lighter side but at the same time keeping on track – having your cake and eating it! This will help you beat your desire and stay focused. Post your goal anywhere you will see it regularly, like maybe the fridge or a mirror, on your wardrobe door you know where is best, you must be able to see it regularly throughout the day.

✓ **Encourage, respect, and accountability**

Explain to a friend or family member what your goal is, including the timeframe, so they can help you with it. This person should repeatedly ask you, how you are doing etc? They should hold you accountable, but at the same time keep you motivated and encouraged. Obviously, they must be the encouraging type! (If not, ask someone else who is) If you are blowing it, they can tell you so, but at the same time gee you up and say things like "Well, that's okay, it's done now, don't sweat it, just get back to it tomorrow." If you are doing well, they can say, "Excellent, well done etc" and make you feel great.

✓ Write and reap the benefits

If you are trying to lose weight your benefits might look something like this: Feel better, better self-esteem, longer life, clothes are more comfortable, a bigger choice of clothes shops to shop it, your husband says you look 25 again and so on. For quitting smoking, it may look like this: Fresher breath, no more brown fingers, less wrinkles on my face, no more red eyes, no more smelly clothes, longer life, and the wife won't make me spend two hours a day on the back porch in the pouring rain anymore! By making a list you will be able to you see what you will receive help from carrying out your goal. Again, it is an innovative idea once you have thought of these benefits to write them down with your goal (On the fridge, mirror etc) so that when you review your goal every day, you'll also see the benefits to achieving it.

✓ You have succeeded – reward yourself!

This can be anything – large or small. If you dropped the fifty pounds, really treat yourself, plan to go out and buy yourself that size 10 dress/or new suit you have always longed for – and then wear it with pride. Make a deal with a partner or friend that if you reach your goal, they will take you out for a meal and spoil you. Whatever it is you plan, make it personal, enjoyable, and desirable to you, so you will look forward to it.

Do not miss this part out – it is one of the most important bits. It will help to keep you motivated when you're struggling and give you something enjoyable to aim for. Make sure you reward yourself for all your hard work! When things get rough, remember; it's the rubbing that brings out the shine in one's soul and the world will endure if there is a spark in man brighter than his everyday wants. Therefore, you have first-hand knowledge about yourself and work hard to make sure it does not become second-hand when you use it. When you put a limit on what you will do, you put a limit on what you *CAN* do. Along your steps to achieving your dream or goal, you will lead or show others how and what to do. You then become a good leader who inspires other men with confidence in him; but you could become a great leader and inspire them with confidence in themselves with your actions and making sure you do things right. Remember our minds are like parachutes - they only function when open, so make sure yours and those around you have their parachutes open to what you want to achieve, not what they want you to achieve.

Remember folks goals aren't just for footballers!
They are for us real people too!

The S.M.A.R.T. Rule

Here is my Simple Law for setting a Goal, I have followed this for many years, and I have found that many other people also use this law. I am unsure as to where I picked it up, so my sincere thanks and gratitude to its creator. I encourage you to pick up a pen and a piece of paper and jot down the goals you want to reach. Look at each goal and evaluate it.

Make any changes necessary to ensure it meets the criteria for a **SMART** goal:

S   Specific
M   Measurable
A   Attainable
R   Realistic
T   Timely

Specific

Goals should be straightforward and emphasize what you want to happen. Specifics help us to focus our efforts and clearly define what we are going to do. Specific is the What, Why, and How of the SMART model.

WHAT are you going to do? Use action words such as direct, organize, coordinate, lead, develop, plan, build etc.

WHY is this important to do currently? What do you want to ultimately carry out?

HOW are you going to do it? (By...)

Ensure the goals you set is specific, clear and easy. Instead of setting a goal to lose weight or be healthier, set a specific goal to lose two centimetres off your waistline or to walk five kilometres at an aerobically challenging pace.

Measurable

If you can't measure it, you can't manage it. In the broadest sense, the whole goal statement is a measure for the project; if the goal is carried out, this is a success. However, there are usually several short-term or small measurements that can be built into the goal. Choose a goal with measurable progress, so you can see the change occur. How will you see when you reach your goal? Be specific! "I want to read three-chapter books of one hundred pages on my own before my birthday" shows the specific target to be measure. "I want to be a good reader" is not as measurable. Establish concrete criteria for measuring progress toward the attainment of each goal you set. When you measure your progress, you stay on track, reach your target dates, and experience the exhilaration of achievement that spurs you on to continued effort needed to reach your goals.

Attainable

When you find goals that are most important to you, you begin to figure out ways you can make them come true. You develop that attitudes, abilities, skills, and financial ability to reach them. You begin seeing previously overlooked opportunities to bring yourself closer to the achievement of your goals. Goals you set which are too far out of your reach, you probably won't commit to doing.

Although you may start with the best of intentions, the knowledge that it's too much for you means your subconscious will keep reminding you of this fact and will stop you from even giving it your best. A goal needs to stretch you slightly so you feel you can do it and it will need a real commitment from you. For instance, if you aim to lose twenty pounds in one week, we all know that isn't achievable.

But setting a goal to lose one pound and when you've achieved that, aiming to lose a further one pound, will keep it achievable for you.

The feeling of success which this brings helps you to remain motivated.

Realistic

This is not a synonym for "easy." Realistic, in this case, means "do-able." It means that the learning curve is not a vertical slope; that the skills needed to do the work are available; that the project fits with the overall strategy and goals of the organization. A realistic project may push the skills and knowledge of the people working on it but it shouldn't break them. Devise a plan or a way of getting there which makes the goal realistic. The goal needs to be realistic for you and where you are now. A goal of never again eating sweets, cakes, crisps, and chocolate may not be realistic for someone who really enjoys these foods. For instance, it may be more realistic to set a goal of eating a piece of fruit each day instead of one sweet item. You can then choose to work towards reducing the amount of sweet products gradually as and when this feels realistic for you. Be sure to set goals that you can reach with some effort! Too difficult and you set the stage for failure, but too low sends the message that you aren't very capable. **Set** the bar high enough for a satisfying achievement!

Timely

Set a timeframe for the goal: for next week, in three months, by fifth grade. Putting an end point on your goal gives you a clear target to work towards. If you don't set a time, the commitment is too vague. It tends not to happen because you feel you can start at any time. Without a time, limit, there's no urgency to start acting now.

Time must be measurable, attainable, and realistic.

Everyone will receive help from goals and aims if they are *SMART*.

SMART is the instrument to apply in setting your goals and aims.

When you get behind the immense success stories in any given field, you often find the most successful have made more attempts and spent longer hours at the given task than anyone else. In other words, they give the law of averages a chance to work in their favour! They just keep on striking out, often against all odds. With achieving goals, this sterling quality of persistence and its bed-fellow perseverance, is essential. Yes, the earlier six steps are also essential and crucial BUT, if you do not persist, your wonderful plan can go down the drain. Your vivid mental images can just evaporate into thin air. Achieving goals simply becomes wishful thinking.

Achieving goals requires that you stay at it day in day out. Then you are **GUARANTEED** results - eventually! To keep this kind of momentum you must develop mental toughness. To be mentally tough means you minimize the effects of discouragement and you turn negatives into positives. Jack Black, in his illuminating book *"Mind Store"*, uses a computer expression to combat negativity *"Delete that Programme"*.

Whenever a negative thought comes into your mind or when others make negative comments, say to yourself, "Delete that Programme" and replace it with a positive thought. For example, when you catch yourself thinking, "This is just not working, this is useless and a waste of time", trigger mental toughness by saying **"DELETE THAT PROGRAMME"**.

Instead think: "What do I need to do to make this work!" Admittedly, negative mental habits are hard to break. It takes time and persistence but oh, the rewards when you do! Just keep on going, **persist, persist, persist,** and let the good old law of averages work for you. Achieving goals **WILL** become your reality!

Remember: The Power of the Mind and Self Belief can change tomorrow and the future. You have the power to change, your Habits and Future.

Mind, Body and Soul All Must Be Tuned

If you were given the choice of choosing the most powerful item known to man, I suspect that at least 80% of humanity would select the Nuclear Bomb. Well, I must disagree, my belief is the human mind to be probably the most powerful force on Earth, and in the Universe as we know it. Without it we are nothing. Combined with our Body and Soul it is truly a remarkable example of the creator's power. Everything that humanity has achieved has been due to one or more minds developing an idea and making it a reality. Without this we would not have the world we have developed at present.

Our duty to use positive thinking to train our minds to overcome assumed difficulties or hardships and even unhealthy habits that we may be experiencing is to free our minds and train them to achieve good habits and positive thoughts. Easier said than done I hear you say, well the Ancient Chinese had methods to be able to clear the mind of rubbish and be as one with the Universe. Yoga and other forms of meditation are an art form that trains the mind to a state of true enlightenment and to grow healthy and strong along with a nurtured body. We need to constantly be aware of the pursuit for a healthy mind, body, and soul, to enable us to be a valuable member of society and an integral part of the fabric that makes up the universe. If your mind set is to be achieving a specified task then you are harnessing the power not only of positive thinking but the power of the universe surrounding you, then your goals will not only be achievable, but reached in the manner and form you wish. To do this takes discipline and dedication and as mentioned persistence, perseverance, and determination to succeed. To block out the negatives that could potentially run you off course or block your road requires you to train your mind steadfastly to the task at hand and keep a clear mind focus. This determination and ambition to succeed is a very precious commodity and needs to be taken care of. If you lose this focus when changing habits or creating your dream or goal, and the steps to achieve this then you have nothing but emptiness and misery. You deserve to reach the highest possible rung on the ladder of life that is open to you, so your ambition and focus must be given the proper attention it deserves.

There are many instances where problems of the mind are raised. These only serve to emphasize the importance of nurturing and training your mind to avoid similar situations befalling you. I expect many times someone has said, *"You must be losing or out of your mind to attempt that."*

This is a negativity and is seen as a statement that you in the opinion of the person discussing this with you, that you are losing your grip on reality. In real terms, it shows they a frightened to try or change their life because of the fear of losing control. This is the key to understanding the way in which your mind, body, and soul work together. This means that once you are no longer in control of your own mind, then you cannot be held responsible for the actions of your body. To show this is when someone performs an act that no-one in their right mind would even attempt. The mind is very much seen as the controlling computer over all our actions.

Positive thinking may not be enough to overcome this level of deterioration but as mentioned meditation or yoga plus other techniques can help you to re-focus your mind and these will halt the downhill slide. A phrase often used and completely misunderstood by many is *"Mind Over Matter"*, this phrase highlights the need in keeping your focus and control of your own mind to overcome any diversity. Although this is but one of the many phrases or sayings around in connection with the mind, they all point to one thing and that is self-control.

Reading someone's mind is seen as a method of channelling and I will not get into that here as that is a whole other area, but it is the ability to read not only your own but another's thoughts and desires or that person's soul. This again emphasises the link between your mind, body, and soul. In so doing it is often thought of as an unwanted invitation into your inner being and raises concerns over mind control(again another area too large to cover here). You think to yourself as you read this, which I am trying to relegate this book to some form of science fiction, a book or movie, but the thought of someone else reading or controlling your mind terrifies a lot of people.

No matter what or who we believe in whether it is God, the Devil, or some other higher power, mind control is seen as invasive and in some cases evil. This is so in the field of Hypnosis, where although the subject is awake and aware of what is happening, he/she has no control over their actions as their mind is being controlled by an outside influence. There have also been cases of mind control by indoctrination as well as by use of drugs and this is far worse and a more brutal attack on a person's mind than anything read in a novel or viewed in a movie.

This area of mind control and outside forces controlling another's thoughts and actions is far beyond my thought processes and also shows just how powerful our mind can be, and yet at the same time be very brittle. My own thoughts are to lose control of your own mind would be worse than losing your legs or arms. We would lose our most precious possession the right to make our own decisions. Thus, if we are not in control and have not got control of our own mind then we lose our decision-making abilities.

Hypnosis used for entertainment is okay as the subject agrees to take part.

To become a fully and integral part of the universe your mind, body and soul must be in harmony, if one of those factors are not under our control then our body is useless to us and we are unable to be decisive, make decisions rationally, re-focus our ambitions, change our habits, in total we are not fully aware of our surroundings and thus muddle through our endeavours as we have for so long up until this time. The main issue I raise here is that we must be in control of our mind to make sure our body and soul are also attuned. Just imagine what the world or the universe would be like if every human being's mind was in full control of their body and soul. The thought of this mega event is enormous and the infinite power it projects is immeasurable. We have conflict and war as well as racial hatred and crime because we are not heeding to our minds. In the World today less than two per cent of the population is harmonised at any given moment. Now for you to be part of that two percent, you must focus on controlling your own mind, empower your body and soul so that you are in full control and no-one or any outside influence can detract you from achieving what you want.

The way to do this is positive, pro-active, make things happen to help you. I hear you saying, "I cannot do that I am not strong enough", defeated before you start. Always start your day, with a smile, look at yourself in the mirror, smile at yourself and tell that true image *"You Love Who You Are, and You Love Yourself"*, this empowers your mind to start the day positive and thus it empowers you.

We must love ourselves and have confidence in ourselves before we can embark on our journey of achieving our goal or dream. I have had you read all the earlier text, to reach this point. The reason you need to see within yourself what has happened, what is happening and what will happen. You control all three and cannot change what has happened but with the power of your mind and self-belief, can change today, tomorrow and your future. The Power is yours, you were born with it and you will die with it. How you use it is up to you. I now say this, it does not matter what favourite items or happenings are, such as that large Pavlova, that kiss from the lady you admire at work, the way someone spoke to you, your first pay cheque. None of this matters if you smile, love yourself and turn all negatives into a positive, or create a positive from a negative.

Negatives or Tension Triggers

We know them; we have suffered them, but how many of us stop, look at the problem and turn it around so the positive comes out. Again, less than two percent do, why? This is an undeniable question and one which many of us shirk for one reason or another. Here are some Tension (Negative) triggers as I call them.

#1 - I can't do that!!!

Are you constantly telling yourself this little phrase when a situation arises? It could be a simple thing as getting up to dance, or going to a party on your own and you know no-one there.

Solution:

Believe in yourself, you can dance; you just need to have the mind set to watch and learn. The party could be a good networking tool to help you gain confidence and new friends. Be yourself, love yourself and above all be confident in who you are. *"There is no such word in as can't."*

#2 – Do feel responsible for others???

Are you always trying to make things easy and keep the peace where others are concerned? Remember doing this and trying to be a peace maker all the time will not make them like you any. All it has done is caused you grief.

Solution: Do the trivial things now and again but if it becomes a habit or they expect you to do it, resist. You are not their servant or slave, empower yourself to be honest with you and them.

#3 – Are you often saying Sorry!!!!

If you have done nothing wrong but say sorry to someone to keep face, or saying to yourself I should not have had that biscuit, or I should not have stayed home today you are being inactive.

Solution: Here is the difference between being active or passive, *"SHOULDS"* never achieve anything and never will. All that word erupts is self-doubt and guilt this then brings on the negatives. Do not second guess yourself be positive, I wanted the biscuit so I had it, I stayed home because I have worked hard and deserved a day off, or I have nothing to be sorry for the blame is not mine. Again, empower yourself be positive and focus on this.

#4 – Criticising yourself constantly!!!

Do you always feel bad about how you look, how others perceive you, how they act towards you, do they make you feel like a fallen martyr and you have not lived up to their expectations.

Solution: You suffer from low self-esteem; you do not love yourself, and if you do not how can anybody else love you. Change your outlook, smile turn any criticisms into an encouragement to do better, visualise what and who you want to be, that will give that positive and fulfilled feeling.

#5 - Perfection !!!

Do you always expect exacting standards and that you are the only one who can do it right.

Solution: No-one in this world and I mean no-one is perfect, not even God. You will never be perfect and to expect that of others is unreasonable. For you to achieve your aims and dreams there must be some give and take. Your focus cannot be that of being the best, this will only cause negativity around you because they are unable to come up to your exacting standards. Realise your limitations and theirs, be positive in the efforts they produce and be thankful and smile that they are helping you achieve what you want as well as maybe feeling good about them.

#6 – To berate one-self!!!

Stop blaming yourself for a mistake, or for being a failure.

Solution: We all make mistakes, and no-one is a failure. Thank the universe for making yourself make mistakes, because when you do make a mistake, you learn a valuable lesson from it. Improve yourself from these experiences and you will feel good about yourself and be in control.

#7 – External Factors???

Are you in control of external factors or do they control you? Are you of the belief that others cause your problems, or do you feel responsible for what others do or say to you?

Solution: You and you alone are responsible to yourself and your decisions and your feelings. People and events do not cause your feelings, but they can affect how you think. Communication is the key in relationships, friendships, and situations. Think positive before making an utterance.

#8 – Hard to receive compliments

Are you always underestimating yourself when you receive praise.

Solution: This is a positive, heed it take it to heart and feel good about it. This shows that you have succeeded in what you have done and by doing such have caused a positive air around you.

#9 – Work under fear or to deadlines!!!!

Can you only produce your best work when under extreme pressure and working to an unrealistic deadline? Because of this are you unhappy, ill at ease and anxious if you do not reach those standards.

Solution: Set realistic goals, realistic steps to achieve them, visualise them, learn more about effective self-assertion. Above all be satisfied with your achievements when you put your goals and steps in place.

#10 – Feeling responsible for someone close becoming annoyed!!!!

Do you say, "it is my entire fault", "I caused this problem",

Solution: Like I have said before you control yourself, similarly others control themselves each owns their own problems. Stop apologising and accepting blame. Everyone has the right to be angry, annoyed, upset but you do not have to feel guilty. Remember that interpersonal conflicts can be healthy leading to constructive change and understanding as well as a positive and brighter outlook.

From the above remember, realise your dreams, create your life in a positive and healthy outlook, as the universe belongs to ***YOU!***

*Remember to reward **YOURSELF***

When achieving certain steps of

***YOUR** goal*

The Importance of Your Soul

The *soul*, according to many religious and philosophical traditions, is the self-aware essence unique to a particular living being. In these traditions the soul is thought to incorporate the inner essence of each living being, and to be the true basis for sapience, rather than the brain or any other material or natural part of the biological organism. Some religions and philosophies on the other hand believe in the soul having a material component, and some have even tried to establish the weight of the soul. Souls are usually considered to be immortal and to exist prior to incarnation. The concept of the soul has strong links with notions of an afterlife, but opinions may vary wildly, even within a given religion, as to what may happen to the soul after the death of the body.

A person's soul is the metaphysical heart, the lifeblood, or the essence of that person. However you prefer to describe or think of it, there is one common belief. It is that the soul itself is non-quantifiable or intangible but is seen as an essential part of every human being. If your mind, body and soul are not in perfect harmony, your life is likely to be, or seem to be, in turmoil. Until this imbalance is addressed, a person's soul is not going to be able to reach the everlasting peace that is its ultimate destiny.

The key to achieving this peace is found through the teachings and disciplines of Yoga. Yoga coaches you through a journey of self-realization and how to unite your mind, body, and soul. This is achieved using various postures, reciting mantras, and meditation. The meditation focuses the mind and relaxes the body that ultimately enables you to examine your soul.

Our eyes are said to be the mirror (or window) to our soul and continued meditation eventually allows us to see into this mirror (or window) and into our soul. We can then work on achieving our mind, body, and soul balance by healing our soul. All believers in the existence of a universal soul are trying to achieve this. We are merely small parts of a far bigger universe. This universe has a soul that includes the souls of all people who have achieved true enlightenment. Enlightenment is the true salvation where your soul is freed from being subjected to further bodily incarnations and it finally becomes an eternal part of the universal soul. Our bodies are the physical manifestation of this cosmic energy and our minds are its intelligence.

We should always use both to ultimately help the Universal soul and not to harm it. Our bodies and minds should be kept as healthy as possible. This will enable us to concentrate on the cleansing of our souls and reaching of course, the link between a healthy body and a healthy mind has long been recognized. If you passionately believe that they are intrinsically connected then it is not unreasonable to take that a step further and link the workings of a person's body and their state of mind with the level of enlightenment that their soul has reached. Our emotions are often associated with our state of mind. If our souls are to join the Universal soul, then our minds, too, must have reached a certain higher state. This is ultimately to have dispelled any negative thoughts and feelings or doubts that we have about ourselves and our destiny. This is all part of reaching your goals. You learn to replace hate with love, hurt with healing, ignorance with wisdom and so on, until all your emotions are beneficial for your soul's quest for peace.

The philosophy of our souls reaching true enlightenment can be aligned with almost any religious or spiritualist belief. We are all striving for the same goal. We want to be welcomed by the higher being or higher power into eternal happiness. Some religions believe that this road is full of bodily reincarnations with our same soul moving through each one until it has achieved its sense of peace.

Others state that each soul only has one bodily incarnation but it is held in a form of limbo until it too reaches the ultimate state where it is allowed to enter the realm of the higher power.

This is why Yoga has such a worldwide appeal as it allows people of all faiths and beliefs to reach a new level of calm and serenity in mind, body, and soul. The journey that a person's soul undertakes throughout a life is no less rigorous than that of the mind or body. In many ways, it is the hardest of all for us to understand as we have no means of measuring the distance that our soul has travelled along the path to perfect peace or how far it still must go.

We can only be sure that the effort and exertion is effective when we see the positive impact that we have on others. An important part of what I am saying here is to be compassionate and positive in our dealings with others. That is something that can be measured and has a truly uplifting effect on the soul. This is how your soul power can be shown to be having an impact on your life. In effect, by showing love and spreading joy you are not only having a positive effect on the lives of others but you are also moving one step closer to the enlightenment of your own soul. Now you can understand that you are made up of three separate parts –mind, body, and soul. Your body and mind are instruments for a higher power that your soul is ultimately looking to join and be free from bodily incarnations. To reach this state of enlightenment takes the union of mind, body, and soul. No matter what your belief system is about a higher power or higher being, the path to true enlightenment of your soul is available to you. All you need is the dedication to seek the balance of mind, body and soul and you, too, can free your soul to join the Universal soul.

In Summary

The Mind

The mind is the control centre of the body and the producer of logical and rational thought. The mind, in this sense, is believed to be either inside the brain or the physical brain is believed to be the control centre of the body, and perhaps an aura or something around the brain or even outside of the head is believed to be the actual thought-producing mind. The brain is essential, on Earth, for communication and the most basic of human function (i.e. walking, talking, etc).

The Body

The body is a structure made of cells that's purpose is to keep the mind and soul on Earth. The body, in this sense can be thought of as something that secures or ties the mind and soul to Earth. The body is often thought of as a vessel for the mind and/or the soul, but there is metaphysical reasoning that suggests that the soul is not a small substance inside the body but rather something that is in no way contained in the body but perhaps intertwined with it. The body ties the mind and soul to Earth, and when the body dies, the tie that secures the mind and soul to Earth is broken.

The Soul

The soul is the elemental human structure that is believed to generate the extremes of human emotion (i.e. love, hate, happiness, etc). The mind and soul together make up what non-religious philosophy refers to as consciousness. In many religious systems, the soul, along with the mind, is believed to be immortal and to live on after death. Many religions believe the soul may become contaminated with sin. Some metaphysical theories suggest that the soul has an image that is visible on Earth; this belief is also associated with the belief that all things on Earth have spiritual qualities.

The dualist model could be adopted and could claim that the body is separate from the soul or the materialist model could be adopted, which supports that there is not a distinction between body and soul.

Remember Our Soul Has

NO

restrictions

Spiritual Growth

It is an important inner process, not only for people who live in far away and secluded places, and who seek spiritual awakening. Spiritual growth is of paramount importance for a better, happier, and more harmonious life, free of tension and strain, fear and anxiety. Spiritual growth is the process of getting rid of wrong concepts, thoughts, and beliefs about who we are and about the world in which we live. Through this process we increase our awareness of our true inner being, the true spirit that we are. It is a process of looking inside us, shedding our illusions, and uncovering our true essence, which is always present, but hidden beyond the ego-personality.

Why should we be interested in spiritual growth? What are the signs that we are growing spiritually? What are the benefits? Here are a few signs and benefits:

- ✓ We develop detachment, which leads to inner peace.
- ✓ We learn not to let outside circumstance affect our moods and states of mind.
- ✓ We become more patient and tolerant.
- ✓ We learn to rise above frustration, disappointment, and negative feelings.
- ✓ Inner power and strength increase.

✓ This process leads to increased feeling of happiness.

✓ Our intuition gets sharper.

✓ We become better citizens of the world.

✓ Our understanding of our inner essence, what we are, and why we are here grows.

How can one grow spiritually? The term spiritual growth is not correct. The spirit is perfect and does not need to grow.

It is a term that describes a process of becoming more aware of what and who we are, growing to look at our life and circumstances from a different, more detached point of view, and of putting things into the proper perspective. It is a process of shedding negative and limiting habits, thoughts, and beliefs, and letting the inner self within us shine out. Imagine a radiant bulb of light, hidden beneath layers of various materials. To let the light of the bulb shine out and illuminate the surroundings, you do not have to strengthen the light or change the bulb.

All you must do is to take away the layers that are covering it. As you remove layer after layer the light shines more radiantly and strongly. How do you remove the layers that are covering the light of your inner self?

You do so through positive thinking, reading spiritual literature, reading spiritual quotes, and by practicing concentration, meditation, and other inner training techniques. If you browse this website, you will find a lot of information, advice, and instructions for spiritual growth.

Here are a few suggestions to start you on the road of spiritual growth:

> ➢ Acknowledge the fact that you are a spirit with a physical body, not a physical body with a spirit. If you can accept this idea, it will change your attitude toward many things in your life.

> ➢ Look inside you and try to find out what it is that makes you feel alive.

> ➢ Try to think positively. If you find yourself thinking negatively, at once direct your mind to thinking on something positive. Open the door for the positive and close it for the negative.

> ➢ Always try to look at the bright side of life. Your inner self is stronger than your circumstances. Don't let circumstances and situations dictate to you how to feel or think.

> ➢ Endeavour to focus your attention on everything you do, instead of letting your attention go wherever it wants.

➢ Start learning and practicing meditation.

➢ Do your best to be tolerant, patient, tactful and considerate.

➢ Thank the Universe for everything that you get.

The philosophy of *No Duality*, or as it is called in India, *Advaita-Vedanta*, says that there is just One Spirit in the Universe, and that everything, living or inanimate, is an inseparable and indivisible part of this One Spirit. No duality further says that it is only illusion, caused by the mind and the play of the senses, which make us regard the world and everything in it, as real and separate from us. For someone not familiar with this philosophy, it might sound strange and even weird, but once understood, it can completely change one's attitude and perspective about life. Imagine a state, in which you feel oneness with the Universe, enjoying bliss and peace of mind, and at the same time acting and functioning normally in your day-to-day life.

A state of being active in the world yet keeping a state of inner detachment. In this state you are aware of your oneness with the One Spirit, and aware that the One Spirit is acting and manifesting through everything, things, plants, trees, animals, and people. This is the experience of no duality in its highest condition.

Ordinarily, the veil of thoughts and the five senses draw the mind outside, to the external world, and obscure the awareness of the consciousness that is beyond the mind. Meditation brings peace to the mind, and develops the ability to silence it, thus enabling us to experience the "state" of no duality. In this state of inner silence, one rises above the illusion of identification with the mind, thoughts, and ego, gets beyond the illusion of separateness, and realizes the oneness with the One Spirit. It is as if a new sort of consciousness dawns, and one sees the world in a unique way.

With this kind of consciousness, we can allow the mind to be active or command it to be silent at our command. It becomes our faithful servant, instead of being our master. We function very effectively in the outer world, yet our basis is in pure, calm, and limitless consciousness, which is not attached to anything and not limited by anything. In this state, we live and view the world from the no duality point of view. Though in our day-today life we refer to other people, as separate from us, this is only a mental viewpoint, convenient for functioning in our daily lives. From a higher state of consciousness, all are One, and the terms "I", "you", "he", "she" and "they" are not real. There is only the One Spirit, Consciousness, which seems to manifest in limitless forms and ways. The concept of no duality is not a strange or weird idea. It can be experienced and lived right here and now, no matter where you are, and without attracting anybody's attention. It is an inner state of consciousness, not an external state. It is possible to realize the meaning of no duality and reach spiritual awakening and enlightenment in an ashram or a cave, and it is also equally possible to do so while living in a town or city with family and job. It is all a matter of fervent desire, inner attitude, and dedication.

Most people cannot afford to live a secluded life to meditate and lead a purely spiritual life. Most of us need to work and support a family and can therefore devote only part of the day to spiritual pursuits. The good news is that we can practice meditation and realize our true being, without abandoning our present style of living. With proper planning, it is possible to find the time and the energy. Meditation, walking on the spiritual path and the realization of no duality can be practiced anywhere, without making external changes in our life. You can stay with your job and family, and still make spiritual progress and realize the true meaning no duality.

Okay, we know you've been bombarded with positive thinking lists - but they really do work, if you work at it. By reading positive thoughts, speaking them aloud, letting them sink into your subconscious they truly start to take effect. So, what have you got to lose by giving it a

go? Absolutely nothing, so why not repeat after us …
again and again and again …

- Appreciate everything that your body can do.
  Every day it carries you closer to your dreams so
  celebrate all the wonderful and unique things your
  body does for you breathing, laughing, sleeping,
  running, dancing, dreaming and add your own
  thoughts here.

- Compile a top-10 list of things you like about
  yourself - things that aren't related to physical
  looks and read it often, at least once a day! As
  time goes by **keep** on adding to it.

- Keep remembering that "true beauty" is not
  simply skin-deep. When you feel good about
  yourself and who you are, you come across with a
  sense of confidence, self-acceptance, and
  openness that makes you beautiful. Beauty is a
  state of mind, not a state of your body.

- When you look at yourself in the mirror or in
  your mind, view yourself as a whole person and
  choose not to focus on specific body parts. Picture
  yourself as you want others to see you all of you
  and not just parts of you.

- Choose to hang out with positive people. It is
  easier to feel good about yourself when you're
  around others who are supportive and who

recognize the importance of liking yourself just as you naturally are.

- Silence those voices in your head that tell you your body is not "right" or that you are a "bad" person. You can overpower those negative thoughts with positive ones so the next time you start to criticise yourself, build yourself back up with a few quick affirmations that work for you.

- Wear clothes that are comfortable and that make you feel good. Work with your body, not against it.

- Become a critical observer of social and media messages. Pay attention to images, slogans, or attitudes that make you feel bad or uncomfortable about yourself or your body. Get active and write a letter to the advertiser or talk back to the image or message.

- Do something good for yourself, just for you! Something that lets your body know you appreciate it. Take a bubble bath, make time for a nap, find a peaceful place to daydream, give yourself a foot massage, watch the sunrise or sunset, dance, sing out loud - keep jotting down ideas. Ask your friends. Share it around!

- Use the time and energy that you might have spent worrying about your body and the way you look to do something to help others. Sometimes, reaching out to other people can help you feel better.

Again, we must look at famous quotes so we can further enhance our thinking and make our goals a more realistic and attainable object, using what we already know and have read:

"A pessimist sees the difficulty in every opportunity; an optimist sees the opportunity in every difficulty."

"The positive thinker sees the invisible, feels the intangible, and achieves the impossible."

"Once you replace negative thoughts with positive ones, you'll start having positive results."

"Instead of thinking about what you're missing, try thinking about what you have that everyone else is missing."

"The pessimist sees difficulty in every opportunity. The optimist sees the opportunity in every difficulty."

Everything in the world of form is preceded by a thought. Thoughts are not in the world of form; form is not in the world of thought. But one precedes the other in all cases. If one wishes to affect form, one must work with cause, not effect. Thought is cause, form is effect. And when we work in the realm of thought, choosing a negative one or a positive one will influence the outcome. Simply put, we live in a world of cause and effect i.e. for every cause there is an effect and every effect must have a cause.

Everything that happens in this world (form) is an effect, the cause being thoughts. These thoughts affect the whole universe. And each thought once generated and sent out becomes independent of the brain and mind and will live upon its own energy depending upon its intensity. All our feelings, beliefs and knowledge are based on our internal thoughts, both conscious and subconscious. We are in control, whether we know it or not. We can be positive or negative, enthusiastic, or dull, active, or passive. These attitudes are supported by the inner conversations we constantly have with ourselves, both consciously and subconsciously. Mystics have long held that we do, in fact, control our reality; not just the trivial things in life, but everything. We create our entire world by the way we think. Thoughts are the causes and conditions are the effects. Our circumstances and conditions are not dictated by the world outside; it is the world inside us that creates the outside.

They have kept that regardless of our circumstances, each person has the innate, Universe or God given ability to create or alter reality to our choosing. This is done by using the power of positive thinking. They say that we are not here to suffer or to live a life of misery but rather, each conflict or problem that we confront is merely an opportunity to express our higher selves, to evolve and to alter the circumstances to our liking. They claim that there is no such thing as a God who looks to punish and that so called errors are merely opportunities to gain experience.

These concepts on the power of the positive thinking, once restricted to the initiated few, came to light in the so-called *New Age*. Voices from people such as Ram Dass, Deepak Chopra, Joel Goldsmith, John Price, L. Ron Hubbard, Dr. Hew Len, and countless others expressed the notion that reality is of our own making and choosing, regardless of appearances to the contrary. The basic premise is that our past conditioning should be re-evaluated and that we should consciously decide the way in which we wish to live. We should use the power of positive thinking to create things (reality) which are good for us and for others. In today's world, more and more people speak about the power of positive thinking. It is a concept that has a remarkably high view of human nature and ability. Its advocates teach that the human mind has the power to turn wishes into reality through optimism.

Positive Thinking

People Can

Achieve Anything

In other words, ***The Power of Positive*** thinking refers to the power of creating thoughts, which create and focus energy into reality. Bring into creation a positive outcome which you see as a benefit to yourself or others. Positive thinking is a mental attitude that admits into the mind thoughts, words and images that are conductive to growth, expansion, and success. It is a mental attitude that expects good and favourable results. A positive mind predicts happiness, joy, health and a successful outcome of every situation and action. Whatever the mind expects, it finds. This is a powerful tool that everybody has, but a lot of people are not aware of it.

"Unlock the Power of Your Mind"

My Life Solutions and Tools

"Do we love ourselves enough to sacrifice something to gain what we want without hurt to the world around us?"

"To achieve your goal is an accomplishment, gratifying, and shows you have achieved your dreams, to help others achieve their dreams is a bonus"

"Turn a challenge into a positive, and then put steps in place to overcome the challenge, learn from the outcome and use it for the future."

Well, I hope you are still with me, and now have some understanding of the *Power of Thought*, *Setting Goals*, why your *Mind, Body and Soul* in harmony is so important, creating new *Habits*, and being *Positive* about yourself. We now embark on the simple steps to create your positive power and some easy-to-use tools to help achieve those goals. From the following you will see how had to adapt to change and re-create new habits, while trying to rid myself of the old ways I had so instilled within me. I never gave up and the support from family and friends was paramount in achieving what I wanted to do.

127

Never ever give up if the road looks too difficult, then stop reassess what it is you want and re-draw the lines. Never go back just use an alternative path. But from the difficulties faced before you change, remember the positives you gained from it, as they will be useful on your new path.

Remember YOU have the TOOLS

Will Power and Self-Discipline

Sometimes, you wish to go for a walk, knowing how good it is for your health and how wonderful you feel afterwards, yet, you feel too lazy, and prefer to watch TV instead. You might know you need to change your eating habits or stop smoking; yet, you don't have the inner power and persistence to change these habits. Does this sound familiar? How many times have you told yourself, "I wish I had will power and self-discipline"? How many times have you started to do something, only to quit after a short while? We all have had experiences like these.

Everyone has some addictions or habits they wish they could overcome, such as smoking, excessive eating, laziness, procrastination, or a lack of assertiveness, we all suffer from this at one time or another.

To overcome these habits or addictions, one needs to have will power and self-discipline. They make a significant difference in everyone's life, and bring inner strength, self-mastery, and decisiveness.

Definitions of Will Power and Self Discipline?

Will power is the ability to control unnecessary and harmful impulses. It is the ability to overcome laziness and procrastination. It is the ability to arrive to a decision and follow it with perseverance until its successful accomplishment. It is the inner power that overcomes the desire to indulge in unnecessary and useless habits, and the inner strength that overcomes inner emotional and mental resistance for acting. It is one of the corner stones of success, both spiritual and material.

Self-discipline is the companion of will power. It endows the stamina to persevere in whatever one does. It bestows the ability to withstand hardships and difficulties, whether physical, emotional, or mental. It grants the ability to reject immediate satisfaction for something better. The human being is full of inner unconscious, or partly conscious, impulses. People sometimes say or do things they later regret saying or doing.

On many occasions people do not think before they talk or act. By developing these two powers, one becomes conscious of the inner subconscious impulses, and gains the ability to reject them when they are not for his/her own good. Will power and self-discipline help us to choose our behaviour and reactions instead of being their slaves.

Don't think that life will become dull and dry in this way. On the contrary, you will feel more powerful, in charge of yourself and your surroundings, and so much happier and more satisfied. How many times have you felt too weak, lazy, or shy to do something you wanted to do?

You can gain inner strength, initiative, and the ability to make decisions and follow them. Believe me; it is not difficult to develop these two powers. If you are earnest and are willing to become stronger, you will certainly succeed.

You will find some exercises and techniques for developing these abilities. These simple, but effective exercises can be performed everywhere and at any time. Go slowly and gradually, and you will see how you get stronger and your life start improving.

There is a misconception in the public mind about will power. It is erroneously thought to be something strenuous and difficult, and that one must exert and tense the body and mind when expressing it.

It is a completely wrong concept.
This is one of the reasons why people avoid using it, though they are conscious of its benefits. They acknowledge the fact that the employment of will power in their life and affairs will greatly help them and that they need to strengthen it, yet they do nothing about it.
Will power gets stronger by holding back and not allowing the expression of unimportant, unnecessary, and unhealthy thoughts, feelings, actions, and reactions. If this saved energy is not allowed expression, it is stored inside you like a battery, and it becomes available at the time of need. By practicing right exercises, you develop

your powers the same way, as a person who trains the muscles to strengthen them.

Developing Will Power and Self Discipline

An effective method for developing and improving these abilities is to perform certain actions or activities, which you would rather avoid doing due to laziness, procrastination, weakness, shyness, etc. By doing something that you do not like doing or are too lazy to do, you overcome your subconscious resistance, train your mind to obey you, strengthen your inner powers and gain inner strength. Muscles get stronger by resisting the power of the barbells. Inner strength is reached by overcoming inner resistance. Remember, strengthening one of these abilities, automatically strengthens the other one.

Here are some exercises:

1) You are sitting in a bus or train and an old man or woman, or a pregnant lady walks in. Stand up and give up your seat even if you prefer to stay seated. Do this not just because it is polite, but because you are doing something that you are reluctant to do. In this way you are overcoming the resistance of your body, mind, and feelings.

2) There are dishes in the sink that need washing, and you postpone washing them for later. Get up and wash them now. Do not let your laziness overcome you. When you know that in this way you are developing your will power, and if you are convinced of the importance of will power in your life, it will be easier for you to do whatever you have to do.

3) You come home tired from work and sit in front of the T.V. because you feel too lazy and tired to go and wash yourself. Do not obey the desire to just sit but go and have a shower.

4) You may know your body needs some physical exercise, but instead you keep on sitting doing nothing or watching a movie. Get up and walk, run, or do some other physical exercise.

5) Do you like your coffee with sugar? Then for a whole week decide to drink it without sugar. Do you like to drink three cups of coffee each day? For a week drink only two.

6) Overcome your laziness. Convince yourself of the importance of what is to be done. Convince your mind that you gain inner strength when you act and do things, despite laziness, reluctance, or senseless inner resistance.

7) Sometimes, when you want to say something that is not important, decide not to say it.

8) Don't read some unimportant gossip in the newspaper, even if you want to.

9) You have a desire to eat something not too healthy. Refuse the desire.

10) If you find yourself thinking unimportant, unnecessary, negative thoughts, try to develop lack of interest in them, by thinking about their futility.

Never say that you cannot follow the above exercises because you certainly can. Be persistent no matter what. Motivate yourself by thinking about the importance of performing the exercises, and the inner power and strength you will gain.

Trying to try too many exercises when you are still a beginner, might end in disappointment. It is better to start training yourself through easier exercises at first, and gradually increase the number and difficulty of the exercises. Practice will improve and increase your power, giving you a lot of satisfaction.

Most of these exercises can be practiced anywhere, anytime. You do not have to devote special times for them. Believe me, they are highly effective. Practicing them enables you to be strong and exercise will power and self-discipline in everything you do. This power becomes available whenever needed. If you practice weightlifting, running, or doing aerobics you strengthen your body. When you need to move something heavy, you have the strength for it. By studying French each day, you will be able to talk French when you travel to France.

The same thing happens with will power and self-discipline. By strengthening them, they become available whenever they are needed. It is important to remember not to choose exercises that might affect adversely your body or health. Deny and give up what is not necessary, futile or is harmful, but not what is vital for your wellbeing. Always use your reason and common sense, so that you do no damage to yourself.

If for the sake of an exercise, you stop doing something that you usually do, and overcome the inner resistance concerning it, you may resume doing it, if it is not harmful. For example, if you love drinking orange juice, and for the sake of an exercise you switch to drinking apple juice, after doing so for some time and after it makes no significant difference for you, you may go back to drinking orange juice, if you still like it. The point here is to develop inner strength, not make life difficult for you and continue doing things you don't like to do.

Advantages of Possessing Strong Will Power and Self Discipline

You need both to rule your thoughts and to be the boss of your mind. The stronger they are, the more control you have over your thoughts, and so your powers of concentration get stronger. When you are the expert in your mind you enjoy inner peace and happiness. Outer events do not sway you, and circumstances have no power over your peace of mind. This might sound too unreal for you, but experience will prove to you that all the above is true. These abilities are essential for self-growth, spiritual growth, and meditation.

They give you control over your daily life, help you improve your habits and behaviour, and they are the keys to every success.

"*YOUR* Thoughts are *YOURS*

They create the world *YOU* want to live in

Be positive and have belief in

YOURSELF!!!"

"all men were created equal.
So you might as well go for
the one with the cash."

Thought Awareness, Rational Thinking

Quite often, our experience of stress comes from our feeling of the situation. Often that feeling is right, but sometimes it is not. Often, we are unreasonably harsh with ourselves or instinctively jump to wrong conclusions about people's motives. This can send us into a downward spiral of negative thinking that can be hard to break.

Thought Awareness, Rational Thinking, and Positive Thinking are simple tools that help you to change this negative way of thinking. The most accepted definition of stress is that it occurs when a person believes that *"demands exceed the personal and social resources the individual is able to mobilize"*.

When people feel stressed, they have made two main judgments: First, they feel threatened by the situation, and second, they believe that their capabilities and resources are not enough to meet the threat. How stressed someone feels depends on how much damage they think the situation can do them, and how closely their resources meet the demands of the situation. Belief is key to this as (technically) situations are not stressful. Rather it is our interpretation of the situation that drives the level of stress that we feel.

138

Quite obviously, we are sometimes right in what we say to ourselves. Some situations may be dangerous, may threaten us physically, socially or in our career. Here, stress and emotion are part of the early warning system that alerts us to the threat from these situations. Very often, however, we are overly harsh and unjust to ourselves in a way that we would never be with friends or co-workers. This, along with other negative thinking, can cause intense stress and unhappiness and can severely undermine self-confidence.

You are thinking negatively when you fear the future, put yourself down, criticize yourself for errors, doubt your abilities, or expect failure. Negative thinking damages confidence, harms performance and paralyzes mental skills. Unfortunately, negative thoughts tend to flit into our consciousness, do their damage and flit back out again, with their significance having barely been noticed. Since we barely realise that they were there, we do not challenge them properly, which means that they can be completely incorrect and wrong.

Thought Awareness is the process by which you see your thoughts and become aware of what is going through your head. One approach to it is to see your *"stream of consciousness"* as you think about the thing you're trying to achieve which is stressful. Do not suppress any thoughts. Instead, just let them run their course while you watch them and write them down on a worksheet as they occur. Then let them go.

Another more general approach to Thought Awareness comes with logging stress in your Stress Diary. When you analyse your diary at the end of the period, you should be able to see the most common and the most damaging thoughts. Tackle these as a priority using the techniques below.

Here are some typical negative thoughts you might experience when preparing to give a major presentation:

- Fear about the quality of your performance or of problems that may interfere with it;
- Worry about how the audience (especially important people in it like your boss) or the press may react to you;
- Dwelling on the negative consequences of a mediocre performance; or
- Self-criticism over a less-than-perfect rehearsal.

Thought awareness is the first step in managing negative thoughts, as you cannot manage thoughts that you are unaware of.

Rational Thinking

The next step in dealing with negative thinking is to challenge the negative thoughts that you found using the Thought Awareness technique. Look at every thought you wrote down and challenge it rationally. Ask yourself whether the thought is reasonable. What evidence is there for and against the thought? Would your colleagues and mentors agree or disagree with it?

Looking at the examples, the following challenges could be made to the negative thoughts we found earlier:

- **Feelings of inadequacy:** Have you trained yourself as well as you reasonably should have? Do you have the experience and resources you need to make the presentation? Have you planned, prepared, and rehearsed enough? If you have done all of these, you've done as much as you can to give a satisfactory performance.

- **Worries about performance during rehearsal:** If some of your practice was less than perfect, then remind yourself that the purpose of the practice is to name areas for improvement and problems so that these can be sorted out before the performance.

- **Problems with issues outside your control:** Have you named the risks of these things happening, and have you taken steps to reduce the likelihood of them happening or their impact if they do? What will you do if they occur? And what do you need others to do for you?

- **Worry about other people's reactions:** If you have put in good preparation, and you do the best you can, then you should be satisfied. If you perform as well as you reasonably can, then fair people are likely to respond well. If people are not fair, the best thing to do is ignore their comments and rise above them.

NOTE: Don't make the mistake of generalizing a single incident. OK, you made a mistake at work, but that doesn't mean you're bad at your job. Similarly, make sure you take the long view about incidents that you're finding stressful. Just because you're finding that new system, or new responsibilities stressful now, doesn't mean that they will *ALWAYS* be so for you in the future.

Keep away from people who try to belittle your ambitions. Small people always do that, But the great make you feel that you, too, can become great.

'Mark Twain'

*Don't let the fear of the time it will take to carry out
something stand in the way of your doing it. The time will
pass anyway; we might just as well put that passing time
to the best possible use.*

'Earl Nightingale'

The Power of Positive Thinking

Positive thinking helps with stress management and can even improve your health. Overcome negative self-talk by recognizing it and practicing with some examples provided.

Is your glass half-empty or half-full? How you answer this age-old question about positive thinking may reflect your outlook on life, your attitude toward yourself, and whether you're optimistic or pessimistic.

In fact, some studies show that these personality traits optimism and pessimism can affect how well you live and even how long you live. Take a refresher course in positive thinking. Learn how to put positive thinking into action. Positive thinking is a key part of an effective stress management strategy.

Understanding positive thinking and self-talk

Self-talk is the endless stream of thoughts that run through your head every day. These automatic thoughts can be positive or negative. Some of your self-talk comes from logic and reason. Other self-talk may arise from misconceptions that you create because of lack of information.

If the thoughts that run through your head are mostly negative, your outlook on life is likely pessimistic. If your thoughts are mostly positive, you're likely an optimist someone who practices positive thinking.

Living longer and happier through positive thinking

Researchers continue to explore the effects of positive thinking and optimism on health. Health benefits that positive thinking may provide include:

- Decreased negative stress

- Greater resistance to catching the common cold

- A sense of well-being and improved health

- Reduced risk of coronary artery disease

- Easier breathing if you have certain lung diseases, such as emphysema

- Improved coping ability for women with high-risk pregnancies

- Better coping skills during hardships

It's unclear why people who engage in positive thinking experience these health benefits. But one theory is that having a positive outlook enables you to cope better with stressful situations, which reduces the harmful health effects of stress on your body.

How positive thinking gives way to negative thinking

But what if your self-talk is mainly negative? That doesn't mean you're doomed to an unhappy life. Negative self-talk just means that your own misperceptions, lack of information and distorted ideas have overpowered your ability for logic and reason.

Some common forms of negative and irrational self-talk include:

- **Filtering.** You magnify the negative aspects of a situation and filter out all the positive ones. For example, say you had a wonderful day at work. You completed your tasks ahead of time and were complimented for doing a speedy and thorough job. But you forgot one minor step. That evening, you focus only on your oversight and forget about the compliments you received.

- **Personalizing.** When something bad occurs, you automatically blame yourself. For example, you hear that an evening out with friends is cancelled and you assume that the change in plans is because no one wanted to be around you.

- **Catastrophizing.** You automatically predict the worst. You refuse to go out with friends for fear that you'll make a fool of yourself. Or one change in your daily routine leads you to think the entire day will be a disaster.

- **Polarizing.** You see things only as either good or bad, black, or white. There is no middle ground. You feel that you must be perfect or that you're a total failure.

Negative sees the hurdles in life, Positive sees the way.

Negative sees the darkest night, Positive sees the light.

Negative dreads to take a step, Positive soars on high.

Negative questions what if ? Positive answers 'I'.

Positive thinking is a mental attitude that admits into the mind thoughts, words and images that are conductive to growth, expansion, and success. It is a mental attitude that expects good and favourable results.

A positive mind predicts happiness, joy, health and a successful outcome of every situation and action.

Whatever the mind expects, it finds. Not everyone accepts or believes in positive thinking. Some consider the subject as just nonsense, and others scoff at people who believe and accept it. Among the people who accept it, not many know how to use it effectively to get results. Yet, it seems that many are becoming attracted to this subject, as shown by the many books, lectures and courses about it. This is a subject that is gaining popularity. It is quite common to hear people say: "Think positive!", to someone who feels down and worried. Most people do not take these words seriously, as they do not know what they really mean, or do not consider them as useful and effective. How many people do you know, who stop to think what the power of positive thinking means?

The following story illustrates how this power works. Joseph applied for a new job, but as his self-esteem was low, and he considered himself as a failure and unworthy of success, he was sure that he was not going to get the job. He had a negative attitude towards himself and believed that the other applicants were better and more qualified than him. Joseph manifested this attitude, due to his negative past experiences with job interviews. His mind was filled with negative thoughts and fears concerning the job for the whole week before the job interview. He was sure he would be rejected.

On the day of the interview, he got up late, and to his horror he discovered that the shirt he had planned to wear was dirty, and the other one needed ironing. As it was already too late, he went out wearing a shirt full of wrinkles. During the interview he was tense, displayed a negative attitude, worried about his shirt, and felt hungry because he did not have enough time to eat breakfast. All this distracted his mind and made it difficult for him to focus on the interview. His overall behaviour made a bad impression, and so he materialized his fear and did not get the job. Jim applied for the same job too but approached the matter in an unusual way. He was sure that he was going to get the job.

During the week preceding the interview he often visualized himself making a good impression and getting the job. In the evening before the interview, he prepared the clothes he was going to wear, and went to sleep a little earlier. On day of the interview, he woke up earlier than usual, and had ample time to eat breakfast, and then to arrive to the interview before the scheduled time. He got the job because he made a good impression. Of course he had also the proper qualifications for the job, but so had Joseph.

What do we learn from these two stories? Is there any magic employed here? No, it is all natural. When the attitude is positive, we entertain pleasant feelings and constructive images, and see in our mind's eye what we really want to happen. This brings brightness to the eyes, more energy and happiness. The whole being broadcasts good will, happiness, and success. Even the health is affected in a beneficial way. We walk tall and the voice is more powerful. Our body language shows the way you feel inside.

Positive and negative thinking are both contagious.

All of us affect, in one way or another, the people we meet. This happens instinctively and on a subconscious level, through thoughts and feelings transference and through body language.

People sense our aura and are affected by our thoughts.

Is it any wonder that we want to be around positive persons and shun negative ones? People are more disposed to help us if, we are positive. They dislike and avoid anyone broadcasting negativity.

Believe in yourself. Have faith in your own abilities!
Without a humble but reasonable confidence in your own
powers, you cannot be successful or happy.

Negative thoughts, words and attitude bring up negative and unhappy moods and actions. When the mind is negative, poisons are released into the blood, which cause more unhappiness and negativity. This is the way to failure, frustration, and disappointment.

"Remember turn a

*Negative into a **POSITIVE"***

Practical Instructions

To turn the mind toward the positive, inner work and training are needed. Attitude and thoughts do not change overnight.

Read about this subject, think about its benefits, and persuade yourself to try it. The power of thoughts is a mighty power that is always shaping our life. This shaping is usually done subconsciously, but it is possible to make the process a conscious one. Even if the idea seems strange give it a try, as you have nothing to lose, but only to gain. Ignore what others might say or think about you, if they discover that you are changing the way you think.

Always visualize only favourable and beneficial situations. Use positive words in your inner dialogues or when talking with others. Smile a little more, as this helps to think positively. Disregard any feelings of laziness or a desire to quit. If you persevere, you will transform the way your mind thinks. Once a negative thought enters your mind, you must be aware of it and endeavour to replace it with a constructive one. The negative thought will try again to enter your mind, and then you must replace it again with a positive one. It is as if there are two pictures in front of you, and you choose to look at one of them and disregard the other.

Persistence will eventually teach your mind to think positively and ignore negative thoughts.

In case you feel any inner resistance when replacing negative thoughts with positive ones, do not give up, but keep looking only at the beneficial, good, and happy thoughts in your mind. It does not matter what your circumstances are now. Think positively, expect only favourable results and situations, and circumstances will change accordingly. It may take some time for the changes to take place, but eventually they do. Another method to employ is the repetition of *affirmations*. It is a method which resembles creative visualization, and which can be used in conjunction with it. It is discussed next.

My Daily Affirmation which you may like to use.

"Today is the beginning of a new start in life.
I have been given this day to use as I will.
I can waste it or use it for my benefit.
What I do today is important because I am exchanging a
day of my life for it.
When tomorrow comes, this day will be gone forever; in
its place is something that I have left behind.
So let today be worth something good.
Thank you, Lord for this day."

The Power of Affirmations

Affirmations are positive statements that describe a desired situation, and which are repeated many times, to impress the subconscious mind and trigger it into positive action. To ensure the effectiveness of the affirmations, they must be repeated with attention, conviction, interest, and desire. Imagine that you are swimming with your friends in a swimming pool. They swim fifteen rounds, something you have never done before, and wishing to win the respect of your friends, you want to show them that you can make it too. You start swimming, and at the same time keep repeating in your mind, "I can do it, I can do it". You keep thinking and believing that you are going to complete the fifteen rounds. What are you doing? You are repeating positive affirmations.

More than often, people repeat in their minds negative words and statements concerning the situations and events in their lives, and so bring upon themselves undesirable situations. Words and statements work both ways, to build or destroy. It is the way we use them that decides whether they are going to bring good or harmful results. Often, people repeat negative statements in their minds, without even being aware of what they are doing. Do you keep thinking and telling yourself that you cannot do something, that you are too lazy, lack inner strength or that you are going to fail?

Your subconscious mind accepts as true what you keep saying, and eventually attracts corresponding events and situations into your life, irrespective whether they are good or bad for you, so why not choose only positive statements?

Affirmations program the mind in the same way commands and scripts program a computer. They work in the same manner as creative visualization. The repeated words help you focus your mind on your aim, and automatically build corresponding mental images in the conscious mind, which affect the subconscious mind. The conscious mind, the mind you think with, starts this process, and then the subconscious mind takes charge.

By using this process consciously and intently, you can affect your subconscious mind and thereby transform your habits, behaviour, mental attitude, and reactions, and even reshape your external life. Sometimes results appear quickly, but often more time is needed. Depending on your goal, sometimes you might reach immediate results, and sometimes it might take days, weeks, months or more.

Getting results depends on several factors, such as the time, focus, faith, and feelings you invest in repeating your affirmations, on the strength of your desire, and on how big or small is your goal. It is important to understand that repeating positive affirmations for a few minutes, and then negatively thinking the rest of the day, neutralizes the effects of the positive words. You must refuse thinking negative thoughts if you wish to reach positive results.

How to Repeat Affirmations

It is advisable to repeat affirmations that are not too long, as they are easier to remember. Repeat them anytime your mind is not engaged in something, such as while travelling in a bus or a train, waiting in line, walking etc, but do not affirm while driving or crossing a street. You may also repeat them in special sessions of 5-10 minutes each, several times a day. Relax any physical, emotional, or mental tension while affirming. The stronger the concentration, the more faith you have in what you are doing, the more feelings you put into the act, the stronger and faster will be the results.

Choose only positive words, describing what you really want. If you wish to lose weight, do not tell yourself "I am not fat" or "I am losing weight." These are negative statements, bringing into the mind mental images of what you do not want. Say instead, "I am getting slim" or "I have reached my right weight". Such words evoke positive images in the mind. Always affirm in the present tense, not the future tense. Saying, "I will be rich", means that you intend to be rich one day, in the indefinite future, but not now. It is more effective to say, and feel, "I am rich now", and the subconscious mind will work overtime to make this happen now, in the present.

The power of affirmations can help you to transform your life. By saying what you want to be true in your life, you mentally and emotionally see and feel it as true, irrespective of your current circumstances, and thereby attract it into your life.

Positive Affirmations

- I am healthy and happy.
- I love who I am.
- Good feelings are pouring into my life.
- I am sailing on the river of health and happiness.
- I am getting healthier each day.
- My body is healthy and functioning in a particularly effective way.
- I have a lot of energy.
- I study and understand fast.
- My mind is calm.
- I am calm and relaxed in every situation.
- My thoughts are under my control.
- I radiate love and happiness.

- I am surrounded by love.

- I have the perfect job for me.

- I am living in the house of my dreams.

- I have good and loving relations with my wife/husband.

- I have a wonderful and satisfying job.

- I have the means to travel abroad, whenever I want to.

- I am successful in whatever I do.

- Everything is getting better every day.

Positive Thinking & Opportunity Seeking

By now, you should already be feeling more positive. Some of your negative thoughts will have been allayed by planning your preparation and contingencies. The ultimate step is to prepare rational, positive thoughts and affirmations to counter any remaining negativity. It can also be useful to look at the situation and see if there are any useful opportunities that are offered by it.

Affirmations help you to build self-confidence.

By basing your affirmations on the clear, rational assessments of facts that you made using Rational

Thinking, you can use them to undo the damage that negative thinking may have done to your self-confidence.

Your affirmations will be strongest if they are specific, are expressed in the present tense and have strong emotional content. Continuing the examples above, positive affirmations might be:

- **Problems during practice:** "I have learned from my rehearsals. This has put me in a position where I can deliver a superior performance. I am going to perform well and enjoy the event."
- **Worries about performance:** "I have prepared well and rehearsed thoroughly. I am well positioned to give an excellent performance."
- **Problems issues outside your control:** "I have thought through everything that might reasonably happen and have planned how I can handle all likely contingencies. I am very well placed to react flexibly to events."
- **Worry about other people's reaction:** "Fair people will react well to a satisfactory performance. I will rise above any unfair criticism in a mature and professional way."

If appropriate, write these affirmations down on your worksheet so that you can use them when you need them. As well as allowing you to structure useful affirmations, part of Positive Thinking is to look at opportunities that the situation might offer to you. In the examples above, successfully overcoming the situations causing the original negative thinking will open opportunities. You will get new skills, you will be seen as someone who can handle difficult challenges, and you may open new career opportunities. Make sure that finding these opportunities and focusing on them is part of your positive thinking.

In the past people have advocated positive thinking almost recklessly, as if it is a solution to everything. Positive thinking should be used with common sense. First, decide rationally what goals you can realistically reach with challenging work, and then use positive thinking to reinforce these.

Choose your response for greater stress relief Lighten your stress load by using responses that help you change your stress level and increase your ability to cope. Feel like you're lugging a backpack that's growing heavier by the minute? That's stress. And too much stress makes life a difficult hike. What exactly is stress? It's what you experience when the level of your stressors exceeds your ability to cope. To balance this equation, you need stress relief by changing the level of the stressors or increasing your ability to cope. Try using one of the four as: avoid, alter, accept, or adapt.

Changing the level of your stressors

Attempt to adjust the sources of stress in your life by avoiding or altering them.

Avoid
A lot of needless stress can simply be avoided. Plan, rearrange your surroundings and reap the benefits of a lighter load.

- **Take control of your surroundings.** Is traffic insane? Leave early for work, or take the longer, less travelled route. Hate waiting in line at the corporate cafeteria? Pack your lunch and eat at your desk.

- **Avoid contact with someone who bothers you.** If you have a co-worker who causes your jaw to tense, put physical distance between you. Sit across the table at meetings or walk around his or her cubicle, even if it requires some weaving.

- **Say no.** You have a lot of responsibilities and demands on your time. At a certain point, you cross the line between charitable and foolish. Turn down the neighbourhood sports league. Pass on coaching T-ball.

- Those around you will appreciate more time with a relaxed you. And you'll have time to enjoy them, too.

- **Turn off the news.** Everyone knows it's the grisly happenings that get airtime. Opt instead to light a candle and read a relaxing book a few days a week.

- **Ditch part of your list.** Label your to-do list with As, Bs and Cs, according to importance. If it's a hectic day, scratch the Cs from your list.

Just remember: A certain amount of avoidance is healthy, but some problems refuse to be overlooked. For those situations, try another technique.

Alter

One of the most helpful things you can do during times of stress is to take inventory. Then try to change your situation, so things work better in the future.

- **Respectfully ask others to change their behaviour and be willing to do the same.** Small problems often create larger ones when they aren't resolved. If you're tired of being the butt of your wife's jokes at parties, ask her to leave you out of the comic lineup. In return, be willing to enjoy her other jokes and thank her for humouring you.

- **Communicate your feelings openly.** Remember to use "I" statements, as in "I feel frustrated by shorter deadlines and a heavier workload. Is there something we can do to balance things out?"

162

- **Take risks.** Sometimes inaction creates tension. Take the art class you've always dreamed about. Vie for the assignment you really want at work. Taking a chance will feel good, regardless of the outcome.

- **Manage your time better.** Organize your day so that like tasks are lumped together — group your phone calls, car errands and computer-related tasks. The reward of increased efficiency will be extra time.

- **State limits in advance.** Be initiative-taking. Instead of stewing over a colleague's non-stop chatter, politely start the conversation with "I've got five minutes to cover this."

Increasing your ability to cope

For those cases in which the source of your stress can't be avoided, try to adjust your ability to tolerate it.

Accept
Sometimes we have no choice but to accept things the way they are. For those times try to:

- **Talk with someone.** You may not be able to change a frustrating situation, but that doesn't mean your feelings aren't legitimate. Phone a friend or schedule a coffee break. You will feel better after talking it out.

- **Forgive.** It takes energy to be angry. Forgiving may take practice, but by doing so, you will free yourself from burning more negative energy. Why swim against the current when you could shrug and move on?

- **Smile.** It may improve your mood. Even if you must fake it, smiles are contagious. Before long, you're likely to see your smile sincerely reflected at you.

- **Practice positive self-talk.** It's easy to lose objectivity when you're stressed. One negative thought can lead to another, and soon you've created a mental avalanche. Be positive. Instead of thinking, "I am horrible with money and will never be able to control my finances," try this: "I made a mistake with my money, but I am resilient. I'll get through it."

- **Learn from your mistakes.** There is value in recognizing a "teachable moment." You can't change the fact that procrastination hurt your performance, but you can register the regret to make sure you allot more time in the future.

- **See stress as an opportunity.** Sure, you're tense, but thanks to stress, you were up early Saturday morning perfecting Monday's presentation. The rest of the day lies ahead, unencumbered.

Adapt

The feeling that you can't cope is one of the greatest stressors. That's why adapting which often involves changing your standards or expectations can be the most helpful in dealing with stress.

- **Adjust your standards.** Do you need to vacuum and dust twice a week? Could a box of macaroni and cheese replace homemade lasagna occasionally? Redefine cleanliness, success, and perfection, and you may use with a little less guilt and frustration.

- **Practice thought-stopping.** Stop gloomy thoughts at once. Refuse to replay a stressful situation as negative, and it may cease to be so.

- **Reframe.** Try looking at your situation from a new reference point. Instead of feeling frustrated that you are home with a sick child, look at it as an opportunity to bond, relax and finish a load of laundry.

- **Adopt a mantra.** Create a saying such as "I can handle this," and mentally repeat it in tough situations.

- **Create an assets column.** Imagine all the things that bring you joy in life — vacation, children, pets. Then call on that list when you are stressed. It will put things into perspective and serve as a reminder of life's joys.

- **Use humour and imagination.** Create ridiculous scenarios in your head. Allow yourself to see an atrocious day as comical. Laugh at the lunacy of it all.

- **Look at the big picture.** Ask yourself, "Will this matter in a year? In five years?" The answer is usually no. Realizing this makes a stressful situation seem less overwhelming.

Choosing the right technique

Obviously, one technique doesn't work for every situation. You can't avoid all the stressors in your life, and you shouldn't accept every hassle that comes your way. Practice appropriately applying these techniques to balance your stress equation. With practice, that once-hefty backpack will become your private bag of tricks. Soon, you'll pull out just the tool that will keep you hiking through life at a steady clip.

Be positive, remember, Nowhere, is

everywhere, if you are not careful.

****

Stress Diary

Finding the Causes of Short-Term Stress

Stress Diaries are important for understanding the causes of short-term stress in your life. They also give you an important insight into how you react to stress and help you to find the level of stress at which you prefer to work.

The idea behind Stress Diaries is that, on a regular basis, you record information about the stresses you are experiencing, so that you can analyse these stresses and then manage them.

This is important because often these stresses flit in and out of our minds without getting the attention and focus that they deserve. As well as helping you capture and analyse the most common sources of stress in your life, Stress Diaries help you to understand:

- The causes of stress in more detail;

- The levels of stress at which you work most effectively; and

- How you react to stress, and whether your reactions are right and useful.

Stress Diaries, therefore, give you the essential information that you need to manage stress.

How to Use the Tool:

Stress Diaries are useful in that they gather information regularly and routinely, over a period. This helps you to separate the common, routine stresses from those that only occur occasionally. They show a pattern that you can analyse to extract the information that you need. Use the Stress Diary and make regular entries in your Stress Diary (for example, every hour). If you have any difficulty remembering to do this, set an alarm to remind you to make your next diary entry. Also make an entry in your diary after each incident that is stressful enough for you to feel that it is significant. The diary can be a normal exercise book or a real diary with one page per day set up. Every time you make an entry, record the following information:

- The date and time of the entry.

- The most recent stressful event you have experienced.

- How happy you feel now, using a subjective assessment on a scale of -10 (the most unhappy you have ever been) to +10 (the happiest you have been). As well as this, write down the mood you are feeling.

- How effectively you are working now (a subjective assessment, on a scale of 0 to 10). A 0 here would show complete ineffectiveness, while a 10 would show the greatest effectiveness you have ever achieved.

- The fundamental cause of the stress (being as honest and aim as possible).

You may also want to note:

- How stressed you feel now, again on a subjective scale of 0 to 10. As before, 0 here would be the most relaxed you have ever been, while 10 would show the greatest stress you have ever experienced.

- The symptom you felt (e.g. "butterflies in your stomach", anger, headache, raised pulse rate, sweaty palms, etc.).

- How well you handled the event: Did your reaction help solve the problem, or did it inflame it?

You will reap the real benefits of having a stress diary in the first few weeks. After this, the benefit you get will reduce each other day. If, however, your lifestyle changes, or you begin to suffer from stress again in the future, then it may be worth using the diary approach again. You will probably find that the stresses you face have changed. If this is the case, then keeping a diary again will help you to develop a different approach to deal with them. Analyse the diary at the end of this period.

Analysing the Diary

Analyse the diary in the following ways:

- First, look at the different stresses you experienced during the time you kept your diary. List the types of stress that you experienced by frequency, with the most frequent stresses at the top of the list.

- Next, prepare a second list with the most unpleasant stresses at the top of the list and the least unpleasant at the bottom.

- Looking at your lists of stresses, those at the top of each list are the most important for you to learn to control.

- Working through the stresses, look at your assessments of their underlying causes, and your appraisal of how well you handled the stressful event. Do these show you areas where you handled stress poorly, and could improve your stress management skills? If so, list these.

- Next, look through your diary at the situations that cause you stress. List these.

- Finally, look at how you felt when you were under stress. Look at how it affected your happiness and your effectiveness, understand how you behaved, and think about how you felt.

Having analysed your diary, you should fully understand what the most important and frequent sources of stress are in your life. You should appreciate the levels of stress at which you are happiest. You should also know the sort of situations that cause you stress so that you can prepare for them and manage them well. As well as this, you should now understand how you react to stress, and the symptoms that you show when you are stressed. When you experience these symptoms in the future, this should be a trigger for you to use proper stress management techniques.

Stress Diaries help you to get a good understanding of the routine, short-term stresses that you experience in your life. They help you to find the most important, and most frequent, stresses that you experience, so that you can concentrate your efforts on these. They also help you

171

to find areas where you need to improve your stress management skills and help you to understand the levels of stress at which you are happiest, and most effective.

To keep a stress diary, make a regular diary entries. For example, you may do this every hour. Also make entries after stressful events. Analyse the diary to name the most frequent and most serious stresses that you experience. Use it also to find areas where you can improve your management of stress.

If you find it difficult to look at your negative thoughts objectively, imagine that you are your best friend or a respected coach or mentor. Look at the list of negative thoughts and imagine the negative thoughts were written by someone you were giving goal advice to and think how you would challenge these thoughts.

When you challenge negative thoughts rationally, you should be able to see quickly whether the thoughts are wrong or whether they have some substance to them. Where there is some substance, take the right action. However, make sure that your negative thoughts are genuinely important to achieving your goals, and don't just reflect a lack of experience, which everyone must go through at some stage.

Summary

Up to this point we have discussed some of the tools that helps you to manage and counter *Stress, Negative Thinking*, etc and how to make your *Affirmations* work and what to do with your *Bad Habits*. We also discussed *Thought Awareness* that helps you to understand the *Negative Thinking*, unpleasant memories and misinterpretation of situations that may interfere with your performance and damage your self-confidence. What *Rational Thinking* is and the technique that helps you to challenge these negative thoughts and either learn from them or refute them as incorrect. To use *Positive Thinking* to create positives that counter negative thoughts. These affirmations neutralize negative thoughts and build your self-confidence. It is also used to find the opportunities that are almost always present to some degree in a tricky situation. Creating will power and self-discipline and how your mind, body and soul must all be in harmony for you to achieve success. The following sections deal with *Self-Esteem, Anger Management*, and learning to say *NO*, and how all this leads to *Self-Confidence*.

Warning: *Stress can cause severe health problems and, in extreme cases, can cause death. While these stress management techniques have been shown to have a positive effect on reducing stress, they are for guidance only, and readers should take the advice of suitably qualified health professionals if they have any concerns over stress-related illnesses or if stress is causing significant or persistent unhappiness.*

"Sort Your Thoughts into Steps of Achievement"

Anger Management

Channelling Your Anger into Performance

Anger can be normal and healthy emotion that helps us instinctively detect and respond to a threatening situation. More than this, when it is properly channelled, it can be a powerful motivating force we all know how hard we can work to remedy an obvious injustice. However, it can also be an emotion that gets out of control, leading to stress, distress, unhealthiest and unhappiness.

Uncontrolled anger can seriously harm your personal and professional life because it can become incredibly destructive to yourself and the people around you. And in a modern workplace that often demands trust and collaboration, it can cause great damage to working relationships.

Understanding the Theory

Anger is a well-developed coping mechanism that we turn to when our goals are frustrated, or when we feel threat to ourselves or to people, things, and ideas we care about. It helps us react quickly and decisively in situations where there is no time for a careful, reasoned analysis of the situation. And it can motivate us to solve problems, achieve our goals, and remove threats.

Acting in anger can serve, therefore, to protect yourself or others. A positive response and constructive outcome can improve your self-esteem and self-confidence.

The Danger of Anger – Foolishness

On the other hand, a negative response can damage relationships and lead to a loss of respect and self-respect. This is particularly the case when we react instantly and angrily to what we perceive to be a threat, but where that belief is wrong. This can leave us looking very foolish.

So, we need to learn to use anger positively, and manage it so that it is constructive and not destructive. Where situations are not at once life-threatening, we need to calm down and evaluate the accuracy of our feelings before, if necessary, channelling anger in a powerful but controlled way.

Anger management, then, is the process of learning how to *"calm down"* and diffuse the negative emotion of anger before it gets to a destructive level.

A Subjective Experience

People experience anger in many ways and for many varied reasons. What makes you angry may only mildly irritate one of your colleagues and have little to no effect on another. This subjectivity can make anger difficult to understand and deal with; it also highlights that the response is down to you. So, anger management focuses on managing your response (rather than specific external factors).

By learning to manage your anger, you can develop techniques to deal with and expel the negative response and emotions before it causes you serious stress, anxiety, and discomfort.

Despite our differences in the level of anger we feel toward something, there are some universal causes of anger that include:

- Frustration of our goals
- Hurt
- Harassment
- Personal attack (mental or physical) on ourselves
- Threat to people, things, or ideas that we hold dear.

We commonly experience these potential anger triggers in our daily lives. A suitable level of anger that is expressed correctly helps us take the right action, solve the problem that is presenting itself, or deal with the situation in a positive manner. If we can learn to manage our anger, we will learn to express it appropriately and act constructively. So, when you're angry, use these 12 steps to calm down:

Step 1: Keep a "Hostility Log"
Use the Hostility Log worksheet to check what triggers your anger and the frequency of your anger responses. When you know what makes you angry, you will be in a much better position to develop strategies to hold it or channel it effectively.

Step 2: If you do, acknowledge that you have a problem managing anger
It is an observed truth that you cannot change what you don't acknowledge. So, it is important to find and accept that anger is a roadblock to your success.

Step 3: Use your support network
If anger is a problem, let the important people in your life know about the changes you are trying to make. They can be a source of motivation and their support will help you when you lapse into old behaviour patterns.

Step 4: Use Anger Management techniques to interrupt the anger cycle

- Pause
- Take deep breaths
- Tell yourself you can handle the situation

- Stop the negative thoughts

Step 5: Use empathy

If another person is the source of your anger, try to see the situation from his or her perspective. Remind yourself to be objective and realize that everyone makes mistakes and it is through mistakes that people learn how to improve.

Step 6: Laugh at yourself

Humour is often the best medicine. Learn to laugh at yourself and not take everything so seriously.

The next time you feel tempted to kick the photocopier, think about how silly you would look and see the humour in your inappropriate expressions of anger.

Step 7: Relax

Angry people are often the ones who let the petty things bother them. If you learn to calm down you will realize that there is no need to get uptight and you will have fewer angry episodes.

Step 8: Build Trust

Angry people can be cynical people. They believe that others are going to do something on purpose to annoy or frustrate them even before it happens. If you can build trust in people, you will be less likely to become angry with them when something does go wrong and more likely to attribute the problem to something other than a malicious intent.

Step 9: Listen
Miscommunication contributes to frustrating and mistrusting situations. The better you listen to what a person is saying, the better able you will be to find a resolution that does not involve an anger response.

Step 10: Be Assertive
Remember, the word is assertive NOT aggressive. When you are angry it is often difficult to express yourself properly. You are too caught up in the negative emotion and your physiological symptoms (beating heart, red face) to put together solid arguments or right responses. If you learn to assert yourself and let other people know your expectations, boundaries, issues, and so on, you will have much more interpersonal success.

Step 11: Live each day as if it is your last
This saying may be overused, but it holds a fundamental truth. Life is short and it is much better spent positively than negatively. Realize that if you spend all your time getting angry, you will miss out on the many joys and surprises that life has to offer.

Step 12: Forgive
To ensure that the changes you are making go much deeper than the surface; you need to forgive the people in

your life that have angered you. It is not easy letting go of past hurts and resentments but the only way to move past your anger is to let go of these feelings and start fresh. (Depending on what, or who, is at the root of your anger, you may have to ask for the help of a professional to achieve this fully.)

These 12 steps form a comprehensive plan to get control of inappropriate and unproductive anger. And the quicker you begin the better. Anger and stress are highly correlated and the effects of stress on the body are well documented.

Key Points

Anger is a powerful force, both for good and bad. Used irresponsibly, it can jeopardize your relationships, your work, and your health. Remember that anger can be creative. People act when they get angry. And providing their actions are constructive, this helps drive change and get things done.

Building Self-Confidence

Develop the Self-Confidence You Deserve!

From the quietly confident doctor whose advice we rely on, to the star-quality confidence of an inspiring speaker, self-confident people have qualities that everyone admires.

Jack Welch once said: *"Confidence gives you courage and extends your reach. It lets you take greater risks and achieve far more than you ever thought possible"*

This powerfully conveys the enormous role self-confidence plays in achieving greater success in whatever you do. Self-confidence is extremely important in almost every aspect of our lives, yet so many people struggle to find it. Sadly, this can be a vicious circle: People who lack self-confidence can find it difficult to become successful.

After all, would you instinctively want to back a project that was being pitched by someone who was nervous, fumbling and overly apologetic? On the other hand, you might be persuaded by someone who spoke clearly, who held their head high, who answered questions assuredly, and who readily admitted when he/she did not know something.

Self-confident people inspire confidence in others: Their audience, their peers, their bosses, their customers, and their friends. Gaining the confidence of others is one of the keyways in which a self-confident person finds success. The good news is that self-confidence really can be learned and built on. And, whether you're working on your own self-confidence or building the confidence of people around you, it's well-worth the effort! All other things being equal, self-confidence is often the single ingredient that distinguishes a successful person from someone less successful.

So how confident do you seem to others?

Your level of self-confidence can show in many ways: Your behaviour, your body language, how you speak, what you say, and so on. Look at the following comparisons of common confident behaviour with behaviour associated with low self-confidence. Which thoughts or actions do you recognize in yourself and people around you?

Self Confidence	Low Self-Confidence
Doing what you believe to be right, even if others mock or criticize you for it.	Governing your behaviour based on what other people think.
Being willing to take risks and go the extra mile to achieve better things.	Staying in your comfort zone, fearing failure and so avoid taking risks.
Admitting your mistakes and vowing to learn from them.	Working hard to cover up mistakes and praying that you can fix the problem before anyone is the wiser.
Waiting for others to congratulate you on your accomplishments.	Extolling your own virtues as often as possible to as many people as possible.
Accepting compliments graciously. "Thanks, I really worked hard on that prospectus. I'm pleased you recognize my efforts."	Dismissing compliments offhandedly. "Oh, that prospectus was nothing really, anyone could have done it."

As you can see from these examples, low self-confidence can be self-destructive, and it often manifests itself as negativity. Self-confident people are generally more positive they believe in themselves and their abilities, and they also believe in the wonders of living life to the full.

Self-confidence is about balance. At one extreme, we have people with low self-confidence. At the other end, we have people who may be over-confident.

Good self-confidence is a matter of having the right amount of confidence, founded and on your true ability. With the right amount of self-confidence, you will take informed risks, stretch yourself (but not beyond your abilities) and try hard. By contrast, if you are under-confident, you'll avoid taking risks and stretching yourself; and you might not try at all. This means that you do not reach your potential. And if you're over-confident, you'll probably take too much risk, stretch yourself beyond your capabilities, and crash badly. You may also find that you're so optimistic, that you don't try hard enough to truly succeed.

So, self-confidence needs to be founded on reality: realistic expectations, your skills and experience, and the effort and preparation that you are willing to put in to reach your goal. So how do you build this sense of balanced self-confidence, founded on a firm appreciation of reality? The unwelcome news is that there's no quick fix or 5-minute solution. The good news is that building self-confidence is readily achievable, if you have the focus and determination to carry things through. And what's even better is that the things you'll do will build success – after all, your confidence will come from real, solid achievement. No-one can take this away from you! So here are our three steps to self-confidence, for which we'll use the metaphor of a journey: Preparing for your journey; setting out; and accelerating towards success.

Step 1: Preparing for Your Journey

The first step involves getting yourself ready for your journey to self-confidence. You need to take stock of where you are, think about where you want to go, get yourself in the right mindset for your journey, and commit yourself to starting it and staying with it.

In preparing for your journey, do the following things:

Look at what you've already achieved:

Relive your life so far and list the ten best things you've achieved in an "Achievement Log." Perhaps you came top in an important test or exam, played a key role in an important team, produced the best sales figures in a period, did something that made a key difference in someone else's life, or delivered a project that meant a lot for your business. Put these into a smartly formatted document, which you can look at often. And then spend a few minutes each week enjoying the success you've already had!

Think about what's important to you, and who you really are:

Next, think about the things that are important to you, and what you want to achieve with your life. (A good way of doing this is to use our Design Your Life workbook to think this through in detail.) Then use a technique like *SMART Analysis* to look at whom and where you are. Looking at your Achievement Log, and reflecting on your recent life, think about what your friends would consider to be your strengths and weaknesses. From these, think about the opportunities and threats you face. Make sure that you enjoy a few minutes reflecting on your strengths!

Think about where you want to go:

Setting and achieving goals is a key part of building self-confidence. Goal setting is the process you use to set yourself targets and measure your successful hitting of those targets. See our article on goal setting to find out how to use this important technique. Inform your goal setting with your *SMART Analysis*. Set goals that exploit your strengths, minimize your weaknesses, realize your opportunities, and control the threats you face. And having set the major goals in your life, find the first step in each. A tip: Make sure it's a small step, perhaps taking no more than an hour to complete!

Start managing your mind:

At this stage, you need to start managing your mind. Learn to pick up and defeat the negative self-talk which can destroy your confidence. And learn how to use imagery to create strong mental images of what you'll feel and experience as you achieve your major goals – there's something about doing this that makes even major goals seem achievable!

Then commit yourself to success!

The final part of preparing for the journey is to make a clear and unequivocal promise to yourself that you are absolutely committed to your journey, and that you will do all in your power to achieve it. If as you're doing it, you find doubts starting to surface write them down and challenge them calmly and rationally. If they dissolve under scrutiny, that's great. However if they are based on genuine risks, make sure you set additional goals to manage them appropriately. Either way, make that promise!

Step 2: Setting Out

Here you start, ever so slowly, moving towards your goal. By doing the right things, and starting with small, easy wins, you'll put yourself on the path to success and the self-confidence that comes with it.

Build the knowledge you need to succeed:

Looking at your goals, find the skills you'll need to achieve them. And then look at how you can get these skills confidently and well. Don't just accept a sketchy, just-good-enough solution look for a solution, a program or a course that fully equips you to achieve what you want to achieve, and ideally gives you a certificate you can be proud of.

Focus on the basics:

When you're starting, don't try to do anything clever or elaborate. And don't reach for perfection – just enjoy doing simple things successfully and well.

Set small goals, and achieve them:

Starting with the small goals you showed in step 1, get in the habit of setting goals, achieving them, and celebrating that achievement. Don't make goals particularly challenging at this stage, just get into the habit of achieving them and celebrating them. And little by little, start piling up the successes!

Keep managing your mind:

Stay on top of that positive thinking, keep celebrating and enjoying success, and keep those mental images strong. You can also use a technique like Treasure Mapping. When you want to achieve something badly, have you ever tried closing your eyes and imagining yourself "there"? You touch it, feel it and see it clearly. You scan every detail in your mind's eye. This is a powerful and important technique for motivating yourself and building the self-confidence needed to achieve your goals. Yet when you open your eyes, the vivid image start fades: it takes real concentration to visualize again each time you want some inspiration.

What if you could keep hold of that vivid image and refer to it whenever you need a little motivation or reminder of what you are working towards? Draw pictures or cut out pictures of your goal or dream from magazines, newspapers etc. On the other side, learn to handle failure. Accept that mistakes happen when you're trying something new. In fact, if you get into the habit of treating mistakes as learning experiences, you can (almost) start to see them in a positive light. After all, there's a lot to be said for the saying "if it doesn't kill me, it makes me stronger!"

Step 3: Accelerating Towards Success

By this stage, you'll feel your self-confidence building. You'll have completed some of the courses you started in step 2, and you'll have plenty of success to celebrate! Now's the time to start stretching yourself. Make the goals a bit bigger, and the challenges a bit tougher. Increase the size of your commitment. And extend the skills you've proven into new, but closely related arenas. Keep yourself grounded – this is where people tend to get over-confident and over-stretch themselves. And make sure you don't start enjoying cleverness for its own sake.

Self-Esteem

Cognitive behaviour therapy techniques can help you unlearn thought patterns that contribute to low self-esteem. See examples of thoughts that can erode self-esteem and learn healthy substitutes.

'Be Proud of Who You Are'

Low self-esteem can negatively affect virtually every part of your life, including your relationships, your job, and your health. But you can raise your self-esteem to a healthy level, even if you're an adult who's been harbouring a negative self-image since childhood.

Changing the way, you think about yourself and your life is essential to boosting self-esteem. Cognitive Behaviour Therapy (CBT) techniques are especially helpful in changing unhealthy thinking and behaviour patterns. These techniques are based on the idea that your feelings and behaviour result from how you think about yourself and your life. CBT techniques can help you recognize, challenge, and ultimately replace negative thoughts or inaccurate beliefs with more positive, realistic ones.

These five steps toward healthy self-esteem are based on cognitive behaviour therapy principles. As you go through these five steps, jotting down your thoughts, experiences and observations in a journal or daily record may help you use these steps more effectively.

Step 1: Find troubling conditions or situations

Think about what conditions or situations about your life you find troubling and that seem to deflate your self-esteem. You may wish to change aspects of your personality or behaviour, such as a fear of giving a business presentation, often becoming angry or always expecting the worst. You may be struggling with depression, a disability, or a change in life circumstances, such as the death of a loved one, a lost promotion or children leaving home. Or you may wish to improve your relationship with another person, such as a spouse, family member or co-worker.

Step 2: Become aware of beliefs and thoughts

Once you've found troubling conditions or situations, pay attention to your thoughts related to them. This includes your self-talk what you tell yourself as well as your interpretation of what a situation means and your beliefs about yourself, other people, and events. Your thoughts and beliefs may be positive, negative, or neutral. They may be rational based on reason or facts or irrational based on false ideas.

Step 3: Pinpoint negative or inaccurate thinking

Your beliefs and thoughts about a condition or situation affect your reaction to it. Inaccurate or negative thoughts and beliefs about something or someone can trigger unhealthy physical, emotional, and behavioural responses, including:

- **Physical responses,** such as a stiff neck, sore back, racing heart, stomach problems, sweating or change in sleeping patterns.

- **Emotional responses,** such as difficulty concentrating or feeling depressed, angry, sad, nervous, guilty, or worried.

- **Behavioural responses,** such as eating when not hungry, avoiding tasks, working more than usual, spending increased time alone, obsessing about a situation or blaming others for your problems.

Step 4: Challenge negative or inaccurate thinking

Your first thoughts may not be the only practical way to view a situation. So, test the accuracy of your thoughts. Ask yourself whether your view of a situation is consistent with facts and logic or whether there might be other explanations. You may not easily recognize inaccuracies in your thinking. Most people have automatic, long-standing ways of thinking about their lives and themselves. These long-held thoughts and beliefs feel normal and factual to you, but many are simply opinions or beliefs.

These kinds of thought patterns tend to erode self-esteem:

- **All-or-nothing thinking.** You see things as either all good or all bad. For example, "If I don't succeed in this job, I'm a total failure."

- **Mental filtering.** You see only negatives and dwell on them, distorting your view of a person or situation or your entire life. For example, "I made a mistake on that report and now everyone will realize I'm a failure."

- **Converting positives into negatives.** You reject your achievements and other positive experiences by insisting that they don't count. For example, "My date only gave me that compliment because he knows how bad I feel." "I only did well on that test because it was so easy."

- **Jumping to negative conclusions.** You reach a negative conclusion when little or no evidence supports it. For example, "My friend hasn't replied to my e-mail, so I must have done something to make her angry."

- **Mistaking feelings for facts.** You confuse feelings or beliefs with facts. For example, "I feel like a failure, so I must be a failure." No matter how strong a feeling is, it isn't a fact.

- **Self: Put Downs.** You undervalue yourself, put yourself down or use self-deprecating humour. This can result from overreacting to a situation, such as making a mistake. For example, "I don't deserve anything better." "I'm weak, stupid or ugly."

Step 5: Change your thoughts and beliefs

The last step is to replace the negative or inaccurate thinking you've identified with exact thoughts and beliefs. This can enable you to find constructive ways to cope and give your self-esteem a boost. This step can be difficult. Thoughts often occur spontaneously or automatically, without effort on your part. It can be hard to control or turn off your thoughts. Thoughts can be immensely powerful and aren't always based on logic. It takes time and effort to learn how to recognize and replace distressing thoughts with correct ones. These strategies may help you approach situations in a healthy way:

- **Use hopeful statements.** Be kind and encouraging to you. Pessimism can be a self-fulfilling prophecy. That is, if you think your presentation isn't going to go well, you may indeed stumble through it. Try telling yourself things such as, "Even though it's tough, I can handle this situation."

- **Forgive yourself.** Everyone makes mistakes. Mistakes aren't permanent reflections on you as a person. They are isolated moments in time. Tell yourself, "I made a mistake but that doesn't make me a bad person."

- **Avoid 'should' and 'must' statements.** If you find that your thoughts are full of these words, you may be setting unreasonable demands on yourself — or others. Removing these words from your self-talk can give you and others more realistic expectations.

- **Focus on the positive.** Think about the good parts of your life. Ask yourself, "What other things have gone well recently?" "What personal skills do I have that have helped me cope with challenging situations in the past?"

- **Re-label upsetting thoughts.** Having negative thoughts doesn't mean you must choose to react negatively. Instead, think of them as signals to use new, healthy thinking patterns. Ask yourself, "Which of my strengths can help me respond in a constructive way?" "What can I think and do to make this less stressful?"

- **Encourage yourself.** Give yourself credit for making positive changes. Treat yourself as well as you'd treat a loved one. Tell yourself, "I did a good job on the presentation. It may not have been perfect, but my colleagues said it was good."

Achieving healthy self-esteem

With practice, these steps may come more easily to you. You'll be better able to recognize the thoughts and beliefs that are contributing to your low self-esteem. Because self-esteem can fluctuate over time, you may want to revisit these steps, especially if you begin to feel down on yourself again. Achieving a balanced, exact view of yourself and accepting your value as a human being may help you feel happier and more confident. And that may rub off on others, too, including your children, family, or friends.

Development of Self Esteem

As Children

Our sense of self, or self-esteem evolves from birth. Between the ages of two and seven we are probably at our most vulnerable as we struggle to understand the difference between ourselves and those around us. In a loving family, a child is supported and encouraged to be the individual person they were born to be.

They are appreciated for the qualities their psychological nature exhibits. But even in a perfect family (if such a thing should exist), our society has clear rules about the types of behaviours which are acceptable. A child does not exist in isolation, but rather part of a family unit where there are not only societal rules, but other complex personalities. At a primal level, the drive of every human being (as in nature) is to survive the environment into which it is born. To do this a child learns to adjust its behaviours to be accepted within the group and in this way, ensure its survival. Depending on the nature of the child and that of the existing personalities within the family, the child may have to change its behaviour by suppressing certain aspects of themselves to receive the love they so strongly desire.

For example, a child who is naturally boisterous and of a dominant disposition may be discouraged from displaying those behaviours if the parents find the child to be troublesome or embarrassing in certain situations.

The likelihood of such displays being squashed is probably higher if displayed by a female as these behaviours are typically associated with maleness. A male child is more likely to be chastised if he were to display what is perceived as a female trait such as crying. Society's rules can have a considerable impact on how much of our true nature we suppress to be accepted within the unit. Children who are shy and sensitive by nature will have difficulty adjusting within a family where these qualities are seen as weaknesses. They may act in ways which hide this part of themselves.

Modelling their parent's response, they too learn to see these qualities in a negative light. The more rigid and controlling the parenting style, the more a child suppresses their original nature to be loved and accepted. The child's first experience of a relationship becomes a model for future relationships as they strive for approval and acceptance.

As Adults

While we may not be aware of it on a conscious level, we are constantly looking for the rules which define the mask we need to wear to achieve approval and acceptance. There are, however, consequences for the betrayal of our original Self. The most obvious is low self-esteem and a niggling anxiety which we often try to ignore. This anxiety results from a betrayal of our *True Self*.

Those who never ask the big question: *"Who Am I?"*, have either been able to keep a large part of their original Self, or are those who are so distracted by the needs of others that they are oblivious to the causes of their stress and anxiety.

This is where anxiety can be a useful tool for those who see it as a sign that things are not right. Rather than a discomfort which should be eliminated with whatever means our scientific world has available at all costs, anxiety connects us to our original fear: that of being rejected. So, when we're in a state of high anxiety and think, "What if I make a fool of myself", "What if I lose control?", "What if they don't like me?" these are the same fears we felt as children or in other situations where we gave up pieces of who we really are to be the person others wanted us to be.

Some people will live and die without ever having asked the question "Who Am I?". There are some people who do not want to delve into the deeper meaning of things. That's OK and their position should be respected because humanity is made up of all kinds of people. But for others, there is an awareness that something is so wrong that simply learning anxiety management skills is not enough. These people are the ones who recognise there seems to be a 'wall' between them and a sense of fulfilment an inner peace. So, what is that wall? What is it made of? In therapy you look at all the things you have had to construct to be the person others wanted you to be. Therapy is about deconstructing that wall.

Persons of high self-esteem are not driven to make themselves superior to others; They do not look to prove their value by measuring themselves against a comparative standard. Their joy is being who they are, not in being better than someone else.

'Nathaniel Branden'

"You are never given a problem you cannot solve"

"A Genius is someone who listens to the light of their soul and obeys"

"Self-Worth is just a state of Mind"

"You deserve as many blessings as you gratefully give to others"

"The quality of your life is based on the quality of the questions you ask"

"Inspired thoughts create inspired dreams"

'Dr John deMartini'

Learn how to say NO!!!!

Am I A Lost Cause Then?

Good question. A lot of unassertive people get caught up in a cycle of behaviour: being over-accommodating, building up resentments, exploding into aggression (the aggression may be internal as well as or instead of external), we dealt briefly on that matter in Anger management, going back to compliance, and then the whole thing starts all over again. Looked at from that point of view it's all about extremes, isn't it?

Compliant and passive at one end of the spectrum, aggressive and attacking at the other end. When you behave primarily at the two ends of this spectrum, you've left out a whole lot of alternative behaviour in the middle that could suit your personality, resolve some tricky issues, and make your life a whole lot easier *So, no, you're not a lost cause!*

What you may have to do is look at how to work in the middle bit of the spectrum to get better, more effective results.

Managing Strong Feelings

It needs to be acknowledged that the strong feelings associated with changing behaviour are real and valid. Once people do that, then these (usually difficult) feelings can be looked upon as a good thing, a sign that something new is happening.

At this point people can start to 'choose' to have these feelings rather than having to endure them or trying to pretend they are not happening. The idea of choice is especially important. If people feel they have real choice about how they behave, they start to realise that it can be OK to put up with something they don't like. They can choose it because they want to; it is to their advantage. They then avoid the disempowering tyranny of always having to assert themselves. (Which is almost as bad as feeling you always must be compliant or nice.)

Many people think that to be assertive, you need to ignore what you are feeling and just 'stand your ground'. In fact, you ignore those feelings at your peril. Often the size of peoples' feelings is way out of proportion to what the situation calls for. They may well reflect an earlier difficult event more accurately. But because that earlier difficulty was so difficult, it feels as though every analogous situation will be the same. It is only by beginning to experience and understand how crippling these feelings can be that people can start to do anything about changing their behaviour.

Many people know what they could say; they know what they could do. Most 'unassertive' people have conversations in their heads about how to resolve a conflict they're in; but still, their mouths say 'yes', while their heads say 'no'. Knowing what to do or say is not the issue here. Therefore, in looking at practising 'the art of saying no', it is wise to broaden the brief to so that it isn't about becoming more assertive; rather it's about changing your behaviour to fit the circumstances.

While in many circumstances assertiveness can be a strait jacket of its own (often creating resistance and resentment), the full lexicon of behaviour can be freeing, because there is choice in the matter. Using charm, humour, telling the truth or even deliberate manipulation, may well get you what you want without having to try behaviour that may go against your personality.

If you add a dash of fun or mischief, 'The Art of Saying No', then becomes a doable prospect, rather than another difficult mountain to climb.

Sure, it's easier to say yes, but at what price to your peace of mind? Here's why saying no may be a healthier choice for stress relief.

Be honest with yourself. Is your plate piled too high with deadlines and obligations that you're trying to squeeze in between meetings? Are you trying to cram too many activities into too little time? If so, stress relief can be as straightforward as just saying no or no more.

Why say no?

There are countless worthy requests out there just waiting to decrease the amount of free time you have and increase your level of stress. So, it's easy to create stressful situations in your life, if you don't turn down requests for your time and talents.

Who will make costumes for the school play or coach your children's Little League team if you don't? The answer may not be simple, but you should still consider these reasons for making sure it's not you.

- **Saying no can be good for you.** Saying no is not a selfish act. In fact, it may be the most beneficial thing that you can do for your family and your other commitments. When you say no, you'll be able to spend quality time on the things you've already said yes to.

207

- **Saying no can allow you to try new things.** Just because you've always helped plan the company softball tournament doesn't mean that you must keep doing it forever. Saying no will free up time to pursue other hobbies or interests.

- **Yes, isn't always the best answer.** If you're overcommitted and under a lot of stress, you've got a much better chance of becoming sick, tired, or only plain old crabby, which doesn't help you or anyone else.

- **It's important to recognize the power of other people.** Let those around you come through. Although others may not do things the same way you would, you can learn a valuable lesson by allowing others to help, while gaining treasured free time.

When to say no!

Sometimes it's tough to figure out which activities deserve your time and attention. Use these strategies to evaluate obligations and opportunities that come your way.

- **Find yourself.** Saying no helps you prioritize the things that are important to you. You'll gain time that you can commit to the things that you really want to do, such as leaving work at a reasonable hour to make time for a mind-clearing run at the end of the day. Examine your current obligations and overall priorities before making any new commitments. Ask yourself if the new commitment is important to you. If it's something that you feel strongly about, do it.

- **Weigh the yes-to-stress ratio.** Is the recent activity that you're considering a short- or long-term commitment? Taking an afternoon to bake a batch of cookies for the school bake sale will take far less of your precious time than heading up the school fundraising committee for an entire year. If an activity is going to end up being another source of stress in your life especially for the long term take a pass.

- **Let go of guilt.** If friends want to get together for an impromptu evening out on the town when you've already scheduled a quiet evening at home with your partner, it's okay to decline their offer. Do what you've set out to do and don't veer off that path because of feelings of guilt or obligation. It will only lead to added stress in your life.

- **Keep your current commitments in check.** If you have relatives coming over for dinner, don't go overboard. Order pizza or ask everyone to bring a dish to share.

- **Sleep on it.** Are you tempted by a friend's invitation to volunteer at your old alma mater or join a weekly golf league? Take a day to think over the request and respond after you've been able to assess your current commitments as well as the new opportunity.

How to say no!

No. Nope. Nah. See how simple it is to say one little word that will allow you to take a pass on the things that aren't a priority? Of course, there are always instances when it's just not that easy. Here are some things to keep in mind when you need to say no:

- **Practice full disclosure.** Don't fabricate reasons to get out of an obligation. The truth is always the best way to turn down a friend, family member or co-worker.

- **Let them down gently.** Many worthy causes land at your door, and it can be tough to turn them down. Complimenting the person or group's effort while saying that you're unable to commit currently helps to soften the blow and keep you in good graces.

Saying no won't be easy if you're used to saying yes, all the time. But learning to say no is an important part of simplifying your way to a better, less stressful life. It also keeps you focused on your goals and the steps you have put in place to achieve that. Saying *No* is part of positive thinking and creating a whole new persona for yourself.

Here are some pointers of what could make

it easier to say **'NO'!**

- ✓ If you're saying something serious, notice whether you smile or not. Smiling gives a mixed message and weakens the impact of what you're saying.

- ✓ If someone comes over to your desk or to your space and you want to appear more in charge, stand up. This also works when you're on the phone. Standing puts you on even eye level and creates a psychological advantage.

- ✓ If someone sits down and starts talking to you about what they want, avoid encouraging body language, such as nods and indications of agreement. Keep your body language as still as possible. Avoid asking questions that would show you're interested (such as, 'When do you need it by?' or 'Does it really have to be done by this afternoon?' etc.)

- ✓ It's all right to interrupt! A favourite technique of ours is to say something along the lines of,

'I'm really sorry; I'm going to interrupt you.'
Then use whatever tool fits the situation.

✓ If you let someone have their whole say
without interrupting, they could get the
impression you're interested and willing. All
the while they get no message to the contrary,
they will think you're on board with their plan
(to get you to do whatever...)

✓ Pre-empt. As soon as you see someone bearing
down on you (and your heart sinks because you
know they're going to ask for something), let
them know you know: 'Hi there! I know what
you want. You're going to ask me to finish the
blah blah job. Wish I could help you out, but I
just can't.'

✓ Pre-empt two. Meetings are a suitable place to
get landed with work you don't want. You can
see it coming. So, to avoid the inevitable, pre-
empt, 'I need to let everyone know right at the
top, that I can't fit anything else into my
schedule for the next two weeks (or whatever).'

✓ Any of these little tips can help you feel more
confident and will support your new behaviour.
For that's what this is: If you're someone whom
others know they can take advantage (they may
not even be doing it on purpose, you're just an

easy mark!) you need to show by what you do that things have changed.

More tips to make it easier to say **'NO'.**

First, it's important to get clear that the vast majority (this means you) of people who don't feel assertive weren't born that way. How many unassertive, accommodating infants do you know? That's good news, because if we follow the logic, it means that you have learned to become unassertive, probably just after the infant stage of your life. This, in turn, means you can learn new behaviours.

Second, we think there are some positive qualities to people who aren't assertive. In all our years of experience, we know that people who aren't assertive tend to be (as we mentioned earlier) sensitive, interested in people, caring, insightful and helpful. These are good qualities to keep hold of, so no throwing the baby out with the bathwater please.

Third, we know that minor changes in behaviour are the ones that will stick when the going gets tough, so that's what we'll concentrate on here.

Fourth, give up the picture that you're going to change over night. You aren't. That's why we recommend minor changes that fit your style, rather than one big, *I'M ASSERTIVE NOW, SO DON'T MESS WITH ME!*

A Few Things to Try

Traditional assertiveness training says, "Just say 'No'" Given everything we've talked about so far, it's hard to do that without coming across as a bulldozer, if you haven't practised it in a long time. Well, we have a few other things you can practise which doesn't involve saying 'no'.

1. Since you're probably already good at apologising, over-apologise. Say that you really, really wish you could help them (whoever the 'them' is) out, but you're so sorry, this time you just can't (do the school run again, stay late, cook for 10 extra people, etc.).

2. Offer solutions - lots of them - that don't involve you. Use your creativity to think of other options that could do just as well.

3. Know a man/woman who can. Pass whatever it is on to someone else, who could do just as good a job as you.

4. Buy time. This is a good technique if you can master it. One of the ways non-assertive people get 'caught' is that they get drawn into someone else's agenda and find it hard to make their own equally (if not more) important. Practise some good time-buying phrases so they roll off your tongue easily:

"I can't give you an answer right now, why don't we schedule a meeting for 4 o'clock."

"I'll ring you back in 5 minutes, I'm just in the middle of something I need to finish."

"I can have it to you by Tuesday at the latest."

"You've caught me at a bad time. I'll get back to you later."

The key here is that none of these are lies; what they offer is time for you to collect yourself, take a breath and decide, out of the heat of the moment, what you want to do about whatever it is you were asked to do.

5. Along with buying time is another simple technique called 'Giving them the good news'. So, while you might say, "I really can't finish this by 6 o'clock," you add, "But what I can do for you is to give it top priority and finish it as soon as I get in tomorrow."

6. Pre-empt. There are loads of situations that you can see coming a mile away (or even a kilometre away). When the phone rings and you hear the familiar 'I'm going to ask a favour' tone, get in there first, "I know what you're going to ask, and I'm so sorry, I already have plans."

7. Confirm where they're coming from: it's always good to let the other person know you understand their point of view.

8. Take yourself seriously. If you're not quite up to that, take whatever is on your agenda seriously.

What I am saying with this list (and there are many, many more trivial things available for you to try) is that in each case they are small, barely noticeable things. When you use one of them, no one is going to accuse you of going on an assertiveness course; they should be practically invisible, except to you. It may feel big to you, but to the outside world, it won't make a ripple.

Another thing to add is that when you try any of our suggestions (in your own words, of course), make a big effort to 'zip your lip' and not go babbling on to make it all right. Say what you have to say, and keep the mouth shut for a reasonable amount of time, till you get a response from the other person. Many times, people will throw away a perfectly good opportunity by talking too much and justifying what they've just said.

To help reinforce your taking steps into the middle of the spectrum, see if you can show a friend, colleague, buddy who will support your attempts at new behaviour. Whenever you get even the smallest 'win' let that person know. It's great to get acknowledgment for even the simplest triumph. This way, you also build yourself up to be able to tackle the real tough ones ("I'm so sorry Mother, this year we won't be coming to Christmas lunch, but the good news is that Frank and I will drive over the weekend before to give you your presents and have a lovely meal together.)

Finally, you aren't alone. Many unassertive people can feel very isolated because their unconfident behaviour is like a magnet for unpleasant things to keep happening. By practising trivial things, in your own time, you, too, will gain confidence and will surprise yourself that you can even begin to 'play' at it when you choose.

"When writing your essays, I encourage you to think for yourselves while you express what I'd most agree with."

"Why do we try to please everyone before ourselves?"

Ask Yourself:

"I am happy with me,
At peace with the world,
And my existence.

What about **YOU** ?"

Self-Efficacy

Although all through this book of solutions we have used differing terms for self-improvement, this one covers them all in a nutshell but again the individual needs to heed the signs of the pointers and information contained in all earlier sections. Self-Efficacy refers to an individual's belief in his or her ability to execute behaviours necessary to produce specific performance attainments. Self-efficacy reflects confidence in the ability to exert control over one's own motivation, behaviour, and social environment.

The strongest source of self-efficacy is mastery experiences, where individuals engage in activities or tasks that lead to successful outcomes. These experiences provide the most direct and powerful way to build confidence in one's ability to succeed and overcome challenges. Self-efficacy can also mean self-confidence, self-assurance but will always be up to the individual as to how they act and in what role.

According to Albert Bandura, individuals form self-efficacy beliefs by interpreting information about their own capabilities.

This information stems from four sources:
- Mastery experiences
- Vicarious experiences
- Verbal persuasion
- Physiological and Affective states.

✓ Mastery experiences provide information about one's successes, but also failures. Generally, successful experiences increase self-efficacy beliefs, while experiences of failure lower them.

✓ Vicarious experiences provide information about modelled attainments of others, which influence one's self-efficacy beliefs by proving and transferring competencies (model learning) and by providing a point of reference for social comparison.

✓ Verbal persuasion by "significant others" can convince people of their capabilities, especially if this persuasion comes from a credible source.

✓ Physiological and Affective states provide information about physiological and affective arousal during situations in which the capability in the domain in question is shown.

In stressful situations people tend to read this somatic information as an indicator of dysfunction, thus affecting negatively on self-efficacy beliefs. Among the four sources, mastery experiences generally have the strongest effect on self-efficacy development, because they are the most authentic indicators of one's capabilities.

Again, it is up to the individual that is YOU, as to how you integrate these four performance attainments as describe by Albert Bandura.

Self-Improvement - *WHY?*

We are *Not* trying to re-invent the wheel.

Following on from self-efficacy why *should* you want:

- to improve yourself?
- Isn't it a sign of weakness?
- Doesn't it prove a lack of self-confidence?

- Aren't you good enough as you are?

In this section, you'll find out why none of these is a valid reason for not taking the path to self-improvement. Sometimes, when all our doubts, fears and insecurities wrap ourselves up, we always come up with the idea of "I wish I was somebody else." Often, we think and believe that someone or rather, most people are better than us.- when in reality, the fact is, most people are more scared than us.

You spot a totally eye-catching girl sitting by herself at a party, casually sipping on a glass of Champagne, you think to yourself,

"She looks so perfectly calm and confident."

But if you could read through her transparent mind, you would see a bunch of clouds of thoughts and you might just be amazed that she's thinking.

"Are people talking about why I am seated here alone?"

"Why don't guys find me attractive?"

"I don't like my ankles, they look too skinny".

"I wish I was as intelligent as my best friend."

We look at a young business entrepreneur and say "Woah… what else could he ask for?"

He stares at himself at the mirror and murmur to himself, "I hate my big eyes".

"I wonder why my friends won't talk to me".

"I hope mom and dad would still work things out."

Isn't it funny? We look at other people, envy them for looking so outrageously perfect and wish we could trade places with them, while they look at us and thinks of the same thing. We are insecure of other people who themselves are insecure of us. We suffer from low self-esteem, lack of self-confidence, and lose hope in self-improvement because we are enveloped in quiet desperation.

Sometimes, you notice that you have an irritating habit like biting off your fingernails, having a foul mouth, and you of all people, is the last to know. I have a friend who never gets tired of talking. And in most conversations, she is the only one who seems to be interested in the things she has to say.

So, all our other friends tend to avoid the circles whenever she's around, and she doesn't notices how badly she became socially handicapped gradually affecting the people in her environment.

*I hope that I'm dispelling any doubts that you might have had. It's important to understand just **why** it's important to improve yourself.*

One key to self-improvement is to *LISTEN* and *TALK* to a trusted friend. Find someone who you find comfort in opening with even the gentlest topics you want to discuss.

Ask questions like:

- *"Do you think I am ill-mannered?"*
- *"Do I always sound so argumentative?"*
- *"Do I talk too loud?"*
- *"Does my breath smell?"*
- "Do I ever bore you when were together?"

In this way, the other person will obviously know that you are interested in self-improvement. Lend her your ears for comments and criticisms and don't give her answers like "Don't exaggerate! That's just the way I am!"

Open your mind and heart as well. And in return, you may want to help your friend with constructive criticism that will also help her improve herself. One of Whitney Houston's songs says, "Learning to love you is the greatest love of all." True enough. To love others, you must love yourself too. Remember, you cannot give what you do not have. Before telling other people some ways on how to improve themselves, let them see that you yourself is a representation and a product of self-improvement.

Self-improvement makes us better people, we then inspire other people, and then the rest of the world will follow. Stop thinking of yourselves as second-rate beings. Forget the repetitive thought of "If only I was richer... if only I was thinner" and so on. Accepting your true self is the first step to self-improvement. We need to stop comparing ourselves to others only to find out at the end that we've got 10 more reasons to envy them.

We all have our insecurities. Nobody is perfect. We always wish we had better things, better features, better body parts, etc. But lives need not to be perfect for people to be happy about themselves. Self-improvement and loving yourself is not a matter of shouting to the entire world that you are perfect and you are the best. It's the virtue of acceptance and contentment. When we begin to improve ourselves, we then begin to feel contented and happy.

Self-Improvement and Self-Growth

Nowadays, the terms self-improvement, self-growth and self-help have become popular. We find many books about these subjects and many websites too. It seems that people are turning inside to find the solution to their problems. They seek knowledge, techniques, workshops, lectures, and teachers who can show them the way.

People begin to understand that self-improvement and self-growth improve the quality of life. The subconscious mind is one of the major keys to self-improvement and self-growth. By changing the contents of the subconscious mind, you change your habits, behaviour, and attitudes. This is brought about through visualization, affirmations, meditation and by analysing behaviour and habits. The process of inner change requires inner work. It is not enough to read, you must practice what you read, and this needs time and effort. There is no such thing as instant self-improvement.

Any inner change takes time, and there must be motivation, desire, ambition, perseverance, and dedication. Outer and inner resistance and opposition must be considered too. Upon starting any self-improvement program, most people usually meet inner resistance that come from their old habits and their subconscious mind, and resistance and opposition from the people around them.

The desire to change, build new habits and improve must be strong enough to resist any laziness, desire to give up and the ridicule or opposition from family, friends, or colleagues. When I saw people with certain traits of character, or a certain kind of behaviour that I did not like, I examined myself to see whether I owned them too. If I did, I visualized and rehearsed in my mind a different sort of behaviour. In my mind's eye I saw myself with the opposite traits of character. I visualized myself in situations, where I manifested the new behaviour.

When I met traits of character or behaviour, which I liked, I used to think about their advantages and benefits and their importance in my life. Here too, I used visualization and affirmations and endeavoured to act in this way in daily life. In this way I have learned and benefited a lot from the behaviour and actions of the people around me, at work, at home, in the street and everywhere else, from people in real life, and from watching people on the screen. It was never for the purpose of judging them or taking advantage of them, but for learning how to act, react and behave in a better way. This process had another benefit. It increased the knowledge about how the mind and thoughts influence the behaviour and actions of people.

Use the following to improve your Self Improvement:

1. Look around you and watch how people behave in various circumstances. Watch the people you meet at home, work, at the supermarket, on the bus, train and on the street. Watch and learn also from people interviewed on TV, and from movies.

2. Watch how people talk, walk, and react, and how they are so treated by others.

3. Pay attention to the way people use their voice and how they react to others' voices. Watch how you feel and act when people shout or speak softly. Watch what happens when people get angry, restless, and upset and what happens if they are calm and relaxed.

4. If you do not like what you see, analyse what and why you do not like it, and then analyse your own behaviour to find out whether you behave in the same way. Be honest and impartial in your analysis.

5. If you discover that you manifest some of these undesirable traits of character and behaviour, affirm to yourself often, that every time you manifest these traits or behaviour, you are going to be conscious and aware of them, and do your best to avoid them.

6. Play in your mind a mental scene of how you would like to behave. Repeat it several times a day, every day.

7. When you detect a sort of behaviour or character traits you like and desire to own, try to act in an equivalent way. Here too, visualize several times each day a scene, where you act and behave in that unique way.

8. You can also decide to change some habit and behaviour patterns and develop new ones, because you believe they are necessary and beneficial, even without seeing them in others first.

9. Think and visualize repeatedly in your mind how you would like to act and behave. Constantly remind yourself of the changes you want to make and strive to act according to them. Each time that you find yourself acting according to your old habit, remember your decision to change and improve, and act accordingly.

10. Do not be disappointed or frustrated if you do not reach fast results. It does not matter how many times you fail or forget to behave as you wanted. Persevere with your efforts and never give up, and you will begin to see how you and your life change.

The Simple Self-Improvement Technique

Self-improvement can turn into an enjoyable, rewarding, and empowering activity. Look at the people around you and watch how they behave. If you find a trait of character or a certain behaviour, which you do not like, examine yourself closely and as impartially as possible, and find out whether you act or behave in the same way. If you do, then think and visualize how you would like to behave in an analogous situation. Then, whenever you have the time, perform mental rehearsals of the new behaviour. Visualize yourself in the same situation, but acting in the way you want to behave.

Think often about the importance and advantages of a changed and more positive behaviour. Tell yourself again and again that you will remember to act differently the next time you are in a situation or circumstances that trigger the behaviour patterns that you want to change. At the first attempts you will probably forget to act as desired but keep visualizing and thinking about the new behaviour patterns, and you will see how you gradually change. Whenever you see people acting in a way that brings them positive results, analyse what they are doing, their body language and the way they are talking and acting, and try to act and behave the same.

If you keep doing so, you will soon start to see changes in yourself and in your life. The advantage of this technique is that you can use it everywhere, anytime, without any prior preparations. Furthermore, this can turn into a pleasurable game. You can use this technique while waiting for someone or something, while sitting on a bench in a park or while travelling in a bus or train. You can use your time more advantageously, instead of just letting the time pass by.

Two examples of this self-improvement technique:

You see one of your co-workers acting angrily. You watch his body language and the tone of his voice and see how people avoid him because of that. Now, look into yourself with an unbiased eye, and find out if you are guilty of the same kind of behaviour. If you are not, that's okay, but if you are, think about the consequences of this behaviour and the advantages of acting differently. Think how a calm and happy attitude can change your life and how people would treat you.

The next step is to visualize yourself in circumstances that trigger the kind of behaviour you wish to avoid, and to see yourself acting in a new and positive manner. Rehearse in your mind, in detail, how you would like to act, so that when you meet this situation, your subconscious mind will guide you to act as you visualized. Mentally rehearsing the new behaviour will remind you to act so in real life and will also motivate and direct you to act accordingly. Here is another example. You enter a shop and ask the saleswoman some questions. She is patient, calm and answers all your questions politely and with a smile.

Her behaviour causes you to feel good and to like her, which may so make you to wish to buy something from her. Analyse the behaviour of the saleswoman and see what you can do to emulate her. Tell yourself repeatedly that you too, are going to behave politely and patiently.

Visualize yourself in various situations that usually make you angry and impatient and ask yourself why you behave in that way. Then start visualizing yourself acting and talking in a calm, polite and patient manner in your day-to-day life. It is important to understand that thinking and visualizing just once is not enough.

You need to do so repeatedly every day, even several times a day, until you see results. The above two examples are only meant to illustrate how to make use of this self-improvement technique. Maintain an open mind, open your eyes, desire to improve yourself, learn from others, affirm, and visualize, and your life will begin to change.

Inner Changes Bring Outer Changes:

The quality of your life depends largely on the quality of your inner emotional and mental life. If you are lazy,

235

worry too much and afraid to try new things, you stick to the same spot. If you are not afraid to change your thinking, your life will soon change accordingly. Your habitual thoughts and the content of your subconscious mind decide your behaviour and the way you act in the world.

When you change the way you feel and think, you ultimately change your inner vision, actions, and behaviour. This causes your outer life to change accordingly.

Some Examples!

If you are the worrying type, you are probably afraid of changes, and prefer to stick to the same kind of life you well know. You see other people who reach success, and though you wish you were successful too, you do nothing about it.

In your mind you see yourself living exactly as you are living now and find it hard to imagine different circumstances. It may never occur to you that you can visualize a different reality. In this case your way of thinking limits you. You constantly see in your mind's eye the same daily reality, and so your conscious and subconscious minds stay programmed to experience and attract the same kind of reality.

Suppose you come to understand and realize that your outer reality is shaped primarily by your inner world. This realization will cause you to aspire to a better life. You will start to envision the kind of life you want to live. If you keep thinking and visualizing a different and better kind of life, soon these thoughts will sink into your subconscious mind and motivate, inspire, and energize you to act. The new thoughts will cause new expectations and change the way you view the outer world. The inner changes in you will gradually affect your outer life. Your behaviour, and the way you act will change. You will have more energy, ambition, and inner strength. You will get over your fear of change and be ready to change and improve your life, by the changes inside you.

Achieving Your Dreams and Goals
Turning dreams into reality

Achieving your dreams and goals depends on several factors and we must keep reiterating these. They are like an affirmation:

1. You should have a specific goal.

2. You must be sure that you really want to achieve your goal.

3. You need to have a clear mental image of your goal.

4. You need an ardent desire.

5. You need to disregard and reject doubts and thoughts about failure.

6. Show confidence and faith and persevere until you gain success

How many people fulfil all the above-mentioned requirements? Just a few! Most people do not know that there are some laws governing success, which should be followed. It is so easy and simple to daydream and then say, "Well it is just a daydream. It will never come true". It is so easy to give up due to lack of faith.

Achieving your goals shouldn't be a tough ordeal. In fact, it can be fun and pleasure, if you go in the right way. It is not hard physical work that brings success. Remarkable success does not require hard physical labour. In fact, you need to do mental work. Visualization and repeating affirmations make up this mental work and are important stepping stones to achieving success. When you visualize and affirm you focus and channel your energies toward your goal. Your mind is geared toward finding solutions to bring your goal into manifestation.

By thinking in a positive manner on your goal, and not letting any doubts enter your mind, your intuition starts working, you see opportunities, and you have energy at your disposal to follow your goals and dreams. Some people listen to subliminal messages, for programming their minds for success. There are many CD's available today, which implant subliminal messages into the mind, to activate its power. Some people prefer to use them because this does not require any effort on their part. It is said that these subliminal messages, which go straight to the subconscious mind, bring faster results. Maybe they do, but then you have no control on what goes into your mind. When you visualize and affirm your goals or write down, you gain much more than just programming your mind passively with subliminal messages. The attention, intention, and energy you channel toward visualizing and affirming, develop in your inner strength, concentration, willpower, and self-discipline. You actively develop your inner powers.

One of the **advantages** of visualization and affirmations is that you can use them wherever you are, at any time, without the necessity of any external instruments. All you need is your mind. Success appears in many ways, sometimes in a miraculous way, sometimes in an ordinary way, and sometimes through an opportunity that appears. A door opens, but you must get in and take advantage of the opportunity.

Correctly following these methods will bring you more ambition, inspiration, and motivation, which would enhance your chances of success. Remember, there are big goals and there are many small daily goals, which visualization and affirmations can make them easier and faster to achieve.

People often erroneously think that goals mean only big goals,

Such as:
- becoming wealthy,
- getting an expensive car,
- having a big house with a swimming pool,
- building a phenomenally successful business.

The truth is that the following are no less important goals:
- getting to work on time,
- spending more time with the family,
- reading a book,
- going to see a movie,
- eating less.

  ✓ How do you visualize and affirm?
  ✓ Are there any special rules and instructions?
  ✓ Yes, there are!

Like any other subject, if you want to do it right you need to study it right. It is simple and easy to learn to achieve success through visualization and affirmations. Anyone can learn to use them right.

Browse the website, and you will find a lot of practical and useful information.

When the mind thinks of success, the outside world mirrors these thoughts.

As the following shows:

- Choose your thoughts carefully; they are the builders of your life.
- Success manifests in small daily events, not only in the accomplishment of great ambitions.
- Happy thoughts make your life happy.
- Miserable thoughts make your life miserable.
- The image you have of yourself handles the way people see and treat you.
- The mental movie in your mind is the cause of everything that happens to you.
- Success is the outcome of thinking, visualizing, planning, and taking action.
- Your mind is the generator of failure, and the generator of success.
- What you think today is what you live tomorrow. Nurturing a feeling of success attracts it into your life.
- Nothing can stand in the way of absolute belief and confidence.

- Your inner world controls your outer world. Learn to improve your inner world, and your outer world would be affected too.
- The mental movie that you play in your mind is the life that you will live tomorrow.
- When you rehearse failure in your mind, you meet failure.
- When you rehearse success in your mind, you experience it in your life.
- Thoughts fuelled by desire and motivation make things happen.
- What you get is decided by the scope of your thoughts.
- Rehearsing success in the mind produces it in the material world.
- Success is not only more money, promotion, and social status.
- It is also more happiness, harmonious relationships, and spiritual growth.
- Change the mental movie that you keep viewing in your mind to one that you like. Keep playing in your mind, and before you know it the movie turns into reality.
- Do not undervalue the importance of success in small matters. It proves to you that with persistence, greater success is possible too.

- Play a movie of success in the projection room of your mind, and soon this movie will turn into reality.
- Your mental movies are the trailers of the future.
- Your thoughts and mental images create your circumstances. Master your thoughts and mental images, and you gain power over your circumstances.
- Attaining peace of mind, happiness, satisfaction, inner strength, spiritual enlightenment and realizing the inner self is spiritual success.
- Attaining good health, love, good relationships, promotion, status, money, and possessions, and realizing desires and ambitions is material success.
- Your outer circumstances are the mirror of your inner world. Change your inner world, and you change your outer world.
- Ambition is the fuel the feed your thoughts, visualization, and actions.
- Willpower, persistence, patience, and work bring your desires into manifestation.
- Visualize your goals clearly, add desire and faith, and you will surely achieve them.
- Attaining peace of mind, happiness and good relationships also mean success.

The difference between **can** and **cannot** are only three letters. Three letters that decide your life's direction. Being positive or negative are habits of thoughts that have an extraordinarily strong influence on life. Always remember the way you think or your circumstances dictate how you feel. The old saying positive and negative are directions. Which direction do you choose? Is so true and positive thinking is expecting, talking, and visualizing with certainty what you want to achieve, as an accomplished fact. Further to this are the following:

- Riches, mediocrity, and poverty begin in the mind.

- Reality is the mirror of your thoughts. Choose well what you put in front of the mirror.

- The mind is the decisive factor in your life, but who decides for the mind?

- A positive attitude brings strength, energy, and initiative.

- To think negatively is like taking a weakening drug.

- Positive thoughts are not enough. There must be positive feelings and positive actions. When you say, "I can't" and expect the worst, you become weak and unhappy. When you say, "I can", and expect success, you fill yourself with confidence and happiness.

- Being resolute, decisive, and courageous in small matters and in big ones is being positive.

- You can close the windows and darken your room, and you can open the windows and let light in. It is a matter of choice. Your mind is your room. Do you darken it or do you fill it with light?

- Positive thinking and negative thinking are attitudes. They are points of view and show the way people handle their affairs.

- Suppose you stand at a crossroads, one way leads to a desert and the other one to lush meadows, which way do you choose?

- Clear thoughts produce, produce clear results.
- Positive thinking evokes more energy, more initiative, and more happiness. Train your mind to think in terms of *'possible'* and *'can be done'*.

- When you have control over your thoughts, you have control over your life.

- Happy thoughts attract happy people into your life. Happy thoughts fill your life with happiness.

- When you change your habitual thoughts, it is like changing the direction of a train.

- Affirm the positive, visualize the positive and expect the positive, and your life will change accordingly.

- When there are difficulties and you feel down, this is the time to visualize, think and expect the positive.

- Do not let circumstances influence your thoughts and moods. By rising over them mentally, you will eventually rise over them materially.

- Fill your mind with light, happiness, hope, feelings of security and strength, and soon your life will reflect these qualities.

- Reading inspiring quotes uplifts the mind.

- Repeating inspiring quotes during the day, helps to cope better with every situation that arises.

- The power of positive thinking is like a car with a powerful engine that can take you to the summit of a mountain.

The mind is like a machine that never shuts down. Does the engine of your car or your vacuum cleaner work incessantly, twenty-four hours a day? Why does your mind work this way? Learn to be aware and conscious of your consciousness, and you will find who you really are. You must learn the power of concentration and this is the ability to focus the mind on one point. There is consciousness of the ego and the world around you, and there is consciousness of the real self, the real you. As you can see there are so many areas of affirmation, inspiration, and words that provoke such positive thoughts and ideas. The biggest thing you must learn though is stop your agitated and negative thoughts and find out who it is that stops them.

Again, concentration and meditation lead to the ability to be without thoughts yet keep full consciousness.

Upon Self-Realization, you will burst into laughter. You will be amazed how simple and different it is from what you have thought it is. To realize your inner self is pure simplicity. You do not have to do anything; yet you must work hard to get it. It may seem a paradox, but it is not.

A Free mind is won by throwing away your mental illusions and attachments. Thoughts are not a necessity; most of the time they are just distractions that obstruct your inner vision. It is possible, through proper means, to teach the mind to think only when it is necessary, for the period you decide.

Without incessant thinking, you become more conscious and alive. People's only genuine experience of the no-thinking state is limited to times of deep sleep (REM) or unconsciousness, as in a swoon or under anaesthetics. Being fully conscious, yet without thoughts, is like sleep, but being awake.

To understand what inner freedom means, imagine the state of the happiness, calmness, relaxation, and peace of mind of deep sleep, but combined with full awakening and awareness.

The waves of the mind lose their power to disturb and distract you, when you still the mind and rise above its desires and whims.
To use the mind when needed, and to switch it off afterwards, is a great art and science. Cleanse your mind with the soap of concentration and wash it with the water of meditation.

Consciousness of your real nature dawns, as you start gaining the ability to still your mind. Peace of mind is experienced when the stormy waves of the mind quell down. Real peace of mind is the companion of the silence of the mind. You get peace of mind not by thinking about it or imagining it, but by quietening and relaxing the restless mind. Silence your mind through concentration and meditation, and you will discover the peace of the Spirit that you are and have always been. The mind is like a TV screen. There is always movement and action there. As you can switch off your TV, so you can switch off the TV screen of your mind. When you sleep, you entertain no visitors at your house, and your windows and doors are closed.

When you want to enjoy peace of mind you have to let your thoughts go and close the windows and doors of your mind. You switch off the engine of your car, so why don't you switch off the engine of your mind? Inner peace creates outer peace.

The mind is like a room that is always full with stuff, there is no free space there, when it becomes vacant, peace of mind prevails, give your brain some rest by switching off the movements of the mind. Stop your thoughts, but stay awake, and you will experience the great ocean of peace beyond the mind. You are the consciousness beyond the mind, by stilling the mind you realize this fact, then peace of mind will always be with you. True peace of mind is not dependent on circumstances, it comes from the inside.

Worries, fears, desires, restlessness, nervousness drive peace of mind away, when you sleep deeply, nothing worries you, you enjoy peace, you can enjoy this same peace while awake and active. Through concentration and meditation, you become the boss of your mind, and gain the ability to tell it when to be active and when to stay silent. You can enjoy peace of mind while talking, eating, walking, working and throughout any other activity, negative feelings and negative thoughts keep peace of mind away. Do you need or enjoy fear, worries and restlessness? If you don't, then why do you keep inviting them into your mind? As the house is cleaned, so the mind can be cleaned. As you enjoy a clean house, you will enjoy a clean and uncluttered mind. When you unclutter your mind, you enjoy peace of mind.

Build a 'Dreams and Goals' Board

Conclusion and Summary

Wishful Thinking – The Lazy Brain's Positive Power

I see too many people who spend life wishing for things. They wish they could win the lottery, they wish they could get a nice new job, they wish their kids would go to university, they wish they had more money, they wish and wish somewhat like a child wishing Santa Claus will bring a new pushbike for Christmas. These people are wishing their lives away, and we all do it at some time in our lives, but there comes a time when we need to grow. The first step from wishful thinking for most people comes when they meet personal development for the first time. Most people then learn the basics for improving their lives.

Positive Thinking and Affirmations

The next step is usually that they (and I) learn the *Power of Positive Thinking* and the *Magic of Affirmations*. These are commonly presented by less knowledgeable lecturers as the magic bullet to turn your life around - rubbish. It is a starting point and a particularly important one but it is not the total solution. *Positive Thinking* means to only think of good things and good outcomes.

Every time you catch yourself with a bad thought you stop it and replace it with a good thought. For example, you are thinking about the surprise meeting with the Boss tomorrow. You do not know what it is about but he has called you in first thing in the morning. Many people would think, what did I do wrong, did he catch me doing X? What added work is he going to lump on me? Positive thinking would replace the above thoughts with I have been doing my job well, he must be giving me a raise!

Positive Thinking alone can be a major factor in life improvement for many people. Those who worry constantly, those who constantly look for the faults and problems in life do benefit greatly from this simple paradigm shift. It tends to happen the more you think about sad things the more they tend to happen.

"In a Gold Mine you can find gold or you can find dirt, it depends upon what you are looking for"

Keeping positive thoughts in mind keeps your outlook and your personality more positive too. This will lead to greater happiness. Think about it. If you spend your time concentrating upon all the terrible things in life, how are you going to feel? If you spend time with good thoughts and good things seem to always happen - how are you going to feel? Positive Thinking goes one step further.

Look for the good in each situation. For example, say your car breaks down and you must walk to an important business meeting. You could curse and swear and lose your temper, get angry and in a huff and storm into the office 30 minutes late and full of venom - how do you think that meeting will go? OR you could think maybe there is a reason for this. What could that reason be? Maybe later you find out there was a traffic jam ahead and you would have been stuck for hours, or you walk the street and find a great special on a home appliance that you have been needing, or maybe you meet an old friend on the way, or a new friend. If you look for the good in a situation you will always find something.

Affirmations are an extension of *Positive Thinking*. *Affirmations* are when you make little sayings to say to yourself every day, some people have their affirmations posted all around the house so that they continually read them. Affirmations are sayings such as "every day in every way my health grow stronger and stronger" or "money flows to me".

This is taking Positive thoughts into the future, you think of the positive things that will happen for you. Again, this is a good reprogramming tool if you are extremely negative and down about your life and prospects but it will not save you, but it is on the path.

Often it is being forced into a demanding situation that makes people look for a solution that they would not have formulated in the first place as they were too complacent. You often see this when someone unexpectedly gets laid off from their job. You see them just after and they are doom and gloom initially. 4 weeks later you bump into them again, they are happy as Larry.

Upon enquiring you find that they now have a better job, closer to home, in a more senior position and the pay is fantastic.

"One door closes, another one opens."

Now the problem with *Positive Thinking* is that people start to believe in it like magic. I once heard a lecturer say *Positive Thinking* only works when you do something about it. Thinking that the grass in the yard was short won't do anything.

This is another problem I see all the time with the *Self Development Seminar Junkies*. They believe that just thinking Positive about a problem makes it go away. Delusional is the word that describes this belief. There is one thing and one thing only that will make your life better and brighten your prospects...

ACTION!!!

That's right getting off your butt and doing something about it. The above tools - *Positive Thinking* and *Affirmations* are a step towards conditioning yourself to action. After years of thinking *Positive Thoughts* and saying *Affirmations* you should have reprogrammed yourself into becoming the sort of person who is successful. The person who is successful is someone who acts. Nothing is going to happen if you sit in front of the TV and think about getting your goals, but if you get out and do something about it **THEN** and only **THEN** will things come to you.

If you make your goals a consuming passion, if you spend all your time chasing the things you love then you will achieve your goals, it might take a while and you will probably have a lot of obstacles in the way but keep your mind on your goals and you will eventually gain them. Even if it takes 20 years at the end would you give it up and go back and live a life you were not happy with.

"Success seems to be connected with action. Successful people keep moving. They make mistakes, but they don't quit"

'Conrad Hilton'

"It is possible to achieve your life's dream if you so desire. Simply act"

'Anthony Robbins'

"Great minds have purposes, little minds have wishes"

'Washington Irvine'

****

Are you a wishful thinker, a positive thinker, or are you an action man? There is absolutely nothing more powerful on this Earth than a person who uses the power of positive thinking and acting. It is the ability to support an optimistic approach towards everything that creates a challenge and to seek the ways to overcome those obstacles without losing focus on the final goal. This book is not the be all and end all this subject. All people start with a goal, but many times are overcome with thinking and dwelling on past failures, instead of looking forward and believing they will ultimately succeed. It is my contention that anyone can achieve anything they wish in this life by only using the power of positive thinking, having their mind, body, and soul in harmony.

Making decisions to change habits, taking the initiative to dream, and set goals. Put steps in place to achieve those goals. Reduce the stress in their life.

Create an atmosphere of positive and rational thinking, where they are relaxed and comfortable with their own existence. Our history is filled with such success stories, and it is never too late to adapt to this philosophy and use the *Power of Positive Thinking*. In one of his many books and articles that I have read on the *Power of Positive Thinking*, **Anthony Robbins'** in the book **"The Power to Shape your Destiny"** offers some interesting ideas on how anyone can choose their own destiny.

I am firm believer in the concept that anyone can choose the path which life leads us down by making the right choices in life, not living in the past, and staying motivated towards a goal. It is the choice of a goal and then following that dream that is the hardest thing for many people to carry out.

The reason, they have not planned or created their universe for it to happen. They also allow negativity to take over and cause them to lose their faith and self-esteem. However, and many times it is quite easy to lose sight or get distracted from completing the tasks.

One concept **Mr. Robbins** covers in his book is called **Transformational Vocabulary**. In it he enlightens us to the power of choosing our words carefully, and how an expanded vocabulary is one way towards moving towards success. It is my contention as well that many people who have a positive mental attitude, should also seek knowledge, and learn to increase their own vocabulary as a part of personal growth. The expanded ability to communicate clearly is just one concept Mr. Robbins eloquently states.

Mr Earl Nightingale in the book *"Lead the Field"* describes the power of the human mind, and how each of us are endowed with the most powerful computer in the world, our own brain. He points out that having a worthy destination and striving each day towards that goal is such a powerful tool.

The power of positive thinking is proved though out this classic book. He begins with describing about the magic word, and that word was attitude. A good attitude is what will be the difference between success and failure, because it the one thing that a person has the most control over.

If a negative image is put forth, the response people will get back is very often the same, however when a smile is given it is often returned. In business or everyday life, the way a person treats other people is often the way they will be treated as well. In other parts of this wonderful book *Mr. Nightingale* often talks about examples of achievement in personal development that have been gained by supporting a positive mental attitude.

This is in fact the single number one point of the book, **"Think and Grow Rich"** by **Napoleon Hill** as well. Human history is filled with success stories of common everyday people who have achieved well beyond their own expatiations by using the power of positive thinking. There are many such authors that author books about positive thinking, it is something that many authors believe to be the secret to true success. It is the cold hard reality of life that often makes most people look at life in a less than optimistic way. Too many times they carry the burdens of other people's problems as well as their own, and it becomes hard to keep a positive outlook. Illness, job concerns and supporting relationships all work against the ability to keep a positive mental attitude about the future for many people.

If, however, they could learn to not live in the past, a place where they have no ability at all to make changes, and instead focus on the present and the future, stress and worry would be reduced significantly. The by-product of this rapidly changing world is stress; it is a primary cause in the rise of medications being used by many people just trying to cope with the pressures. If those same people could keep a happy, optimistic outlook, the world would surely be a much better place to co-exist in. Reading and listening to others talk about a positive attitude is one thing, but it must be an action taken by the individual for the power of change to happen.

Destiny is in a constant state of flux and can be changed by simple actions starting right now and is something anyone can do with just a little effort. Again, to think positive, create a stress-free environment and put steps in place to achieve your goal which leads you to you your selected Destiny, is all self-created.

No-One can create or manufacture your Destiny. It is my contention that no one should lead a life of despair and desperation. The power to make changes in anyone's life can be easily carried out with the *Power of Positive Thinking*.

From **Henry Ford** to **Thomas Edison**, and many of the other great innovators in our world had just one thing in common, they all kept a positive outlook on their own destiny, and they stayed the course with determination and refused to let life bring them down or let someone tell them they could not do anything they wanted to do. This is the gift we all share and sadly many people do not even know they have the ability already.

No training is needed, no special tools need be acquired, just use the power of the brain and choose to be a positive person on this Earth. It is the only way that they will be able to know exactly what purpose they were born to achieve in this life. The answers to all the questions are already inside our minds, just waiting to be unlocked, using the power of positive thinking.

Remember we all own that is each individual walking in this great Universe the most powerful piece of equipment known to man, yet it was not created by man. The item is our brain, the computer of our existence. It has been proven that we use the smallest area of this vast piece of equipment. Yet our brain can create almost anything and solve any problem presented, put a man on the moon, create the Atomic Bomb, unravelled the mysteries of the Universe and much, much more. With this amount of power, it is but a small surge of energy to create our future as we wish and desire it to be.

The Following Never Change:

1. **Every Living Human Being Has Problems.**

   Perhaps you are unhappy with your work. Isn't it good that you have a job rather than being unemployed? Many people have the mistaken notion that successful people do not have any problems. It is not true. Success tends to breed its own set of problems. Everyone has problems. A problem-free life is an illusion - a mirage in the desert. Accept the fact that everyone has problems. This will help you to move on with your life rather than sitting and feeling pity for yourself.

2. **Every Problem Has a Limited Life Span**

Every mountain has a peak and every valley has a low point. Similarly, life has its ups and downs. No one is up all the time or down all the time. Problems do get resolved in the long term. They don't last forever. History teaches that every problem has a limited life span. Your problems will not live forever; but you will! Storms are followed by sunshine. Winter is followed by spring. Your problems will get resolved given enough time.

3. Every Problem Holds Positive Possibilities

There are two sides to every coin. What may be a problem for one could be interesting opportunity to someone else. Hospitals are there because people get sick; garages are there because cars do break down; lawyers are there because people get in trouble with the law occasionally. Every cloud has a silver lining.

4. Every Problem Will Change You

When me meet problems head on in life, they leave their indelible mark on us. The experience could make you better or worse. It is up to you. What is certain is that problems never leave us the same way they found us. We will change. For example, let us say that you lost your job. You can sit and feel sorry for yourself. Or you can be aggressive and decide to do something about it. You are better than them. You want to show them what a mistake they did in firing you. You must be fired before you can be fired up. That may be wake-up call you needed before embarking on a successful mission. Again, for every problem, there is a positive and negative side. Look for the positive side and work on it.

5. **You Can Choose What Your Problem Will Do to You**

You may not be able to control the problems, but you certainly can control your reaction or response to the problem. You can turn your pain into profanity or into poetry. The choice is up to you. You can control the reaction even if you cannot control the problem. You control the effect of the problem by controlling the reaction. It can make you tough or tender. It can make you better or bitter. It all depends on you.

6. **There Is a Negative and a Positive Reaction to Every Problem**

Tough people, according to most experts, have learned to choose the most positive reaction in managing problems. The key is that they manage their problems.

Remember, we have little control on problems; we have control on how we react and manage the problem. Positive people chose to react positively to their predicaments.

> Do you automatically interpret silence on the part of your spouse to mean anger when it could just as easily mean fatigue?

> Do you blame yourself when a sudden downpour drenches your wash on the line?

> Do you dwell on the few times your boss criticized your performance and ignore the innumerable times s/he's praised you?

> We all fall into the negative thinking rut from time to time.

> We badger ourselves with "should haves" and lose sight of the fact that "good" and "bad" in life is rarely black and white.

> All-or-nothing thinking can lead to anxiety, depression, and feelings of inferiority, perfectionism, and anger. We are our worst enemies.

- ➤ We tend to put a higher standard for us compared to others.

- ➤ We tend to criticize ourselves for our miscues rather than being happy for the accomplishments.

- ➤ Allow yourself to fail now and then. It's all part of being human.

Remember a problem is not a problem just a positive in reverse!!!

Learning To Like and Love Ourselves

The messages we receive from other people and from the media are largely negative. Unwelcome news gets more attention than good news. This seeps into our day-to-day lives as well. If we admire some aspect of ourselves, we are seen to be conceited. If we say negative things about ourselves, people will console us.

We were rewarded for misery since our childhood; we are offered candy or hugs when we are unhappy. No rewards for our laughter and happiness! Some people like the attention and sympathy. So, they purposely distort the facts and tell others all the troubles and miseries they have. After some time, their sub-conscious mind will start believing what they are saying and start acting accordingly.

Soon they will have reasons to be unhappy for real. Do not get into this trap. See the positive rather than the negative in you. Optimism and a positive attitude promote good health. Research shows that the optimistic persons have healthier immune system. Pessimistic expectations breed negative experiences. How can you incorporate these into your own life? Be grateful. No matter how terrible things might appear, you can see a silver lining.

➤ There is someone who has worse problems.

- Misery loves companions.
- Reach out to such people.
- This will help both parties.
- Make a conscious effort towards finding good things.
- As far as possible stay away from pessimistic people.
- Don't get drawn into other people's misery.
- Catch yourself if you are whining and stop.
- Your stress levels will benefit at once.
- We all can make a deliberate choice between being negative or positive, happy, or unhappy.

Say and believe in the following:

- *You are unique.*
- *There is no one like you in the entire world.*
- *Enjoy and cherish the feeling that you are special.*
- *Remember your successes when you are feeling defeated.*

We have many ways of reconnecting to our inner and outer selves. We must only stay still long enough to allow it to happen. In the words of *Jon Kabat-Zinn*, author of *'wherever you go, there you are:'*

"Letting go means just what it says. It's an invitation to cease clinging to anything – whether it be an idea, a thing, an event, a particular time, a view, or desire. It is a conscious decision to release with full acceptance into the stream of present moments as they are unfolding. To let go means to give up coercing, resisting, or struggling, in exchange for something more powerful and wholesome which comes out of allowing things to be as they are."

Watching your breath as it goes in and out is an excellent starting place for this practice of letting go. As you allow your body to "breathe itself," interesting things start to happen. Gradually, the "out there" becomes "in here" and the "in here" becomes "out there." "I" becomes "we," and "we" become "one" as boundaries fade and disappear. For a moment, we slip into that space between the worlds. We have shifted from human "doing" to human "being." Even done briefly, this awareness exercise is amazingly refreshing, revitalizing, and awakening in more ways than one.

Our habitual patterns become clearer, and we start to see choices in our beliefs and responses. Reality is not what it used to be! We notice that maybe the boss didn't mean to be critical, he was just having a rough day. Or the attractive guy or woman in the next office is smiling at you and meaning it, and not just being polite as you had previously thought. By slowing down, you have practiced a sharpening of your inner and outer feelings, with better understanding of yourself and those around you. Your intuition may be sharper. You may even find yourself saying 'no' to an unwanted assignment, and not even feel guilty about it.

These are a few steps I recommend helping you with creating a healthy Body, Mind and Soul

- Plan ahead

- Make a to-do list in order of priorities

- Don't try to pack more into your day than you can cope with comfortably.

- Finish the most important task before you tackle the next one.

- Do not bite off more than you can chew.

- Just say 'no' to unrealistic deadlines.

- There is no need to feel guilty if you must change plans or arrangements because of an impossibly tight schedule.

- Take regular breaks. Short rests between periods of concentrated mental effort, particularly when you are frustrated with a project or are unable to move forward, can be refreshing and help you to refocus. Five minutes of each hour or 15 minutes every two hours allows a more manageable pace.

- Take regular Holidays

- Stop Living Beyond Your Means: Living beyond your means can make you sick. A researcher at the University of Oxford studied British census data on 20,000 households and found that families that tried to keep lifestyles they couldn't afford were likely to have health problems.

- Sit up straight. A good upright posture improves breathing and increases blood flow to the brain. We often slouch when stressed, which restricts breathing and blood flow and can magnify feelings of helplessness.

- Learn to recognize your own symptoms of stress. These may include irritability, sleeplessness, social and/or sexual withdrawal, loss of interest in activities, and lack of appetite.

- Talk about stressful events to a friend or spouse before you reach a breaking point. If you can, let go and cry. Like talking, crying externalizes pent-up feelings and may reduce the risk of stress-related illness. If you need extra help, seek counselling from a mental health professional.

- Recognize that some things cannot be changed and put your energy toward those that can.

- Find the sources of your stress. This gives you more choice in how you react. If necessary, make a note of the circumstances, and see if a pattern appears. As you delve deeper, you are more likely to discover the root of your problem. This will allow you to solve it at the deepest, most effective level.

- Cultivate an optimistic attitude. Don't talk yourself into believing that you can't cope.

- Reduce your exposure to events that make you angry. Go to the bank at an off-hour to avoid maddening lines. Mask outside noise by turning on relaxing music.

- Maintain a sense of humour about it all.

- Learn to express anger in a constructive way. Keeping anger within you adds to feelings of stress; blowing up in a rage is almost as bad. Simply being able to say, *"that makes me very angry"* and working out ways of avoiding anger-provoking situations are positive steps in dealing with anger.

- Focus on others' rather than your own problems. If time allows, do a few hours of volunteer work each week.

- Exercise every day, even if you have time for only a brisk, 20-minute walk.

- Stretch your chest for better breathing: The tense musculature of a person under stress can make breathing difficult and impaired breathing can aggravate the anxiety you already feel. To relax your breathing, roll your shoulders up and back then relax. The first time, inhale deeply as they go back, exhale as they relax. Repeat four or five more times, then inhale deeply again. Repeat the entire sequence four times.

- Get a Hand Exerciser: Keep a hand exerciser or a tennis ball in your desk at work and give it a few squeezes during tense times. When stress shoots adrenaline into the bloodstream that calls for muscle action. Squeezing something provides a release that satisfies our bodies' fight-or-flee response.

- Pop a bubble. A study found that students were able to reduce their feelings of tension by popping two sheets of those plastic air capsules used in packaging.

- Soak in the Tub: Soaking in hot tub is an exceptionally good stress-reliever. We have covered this in detail elsewhere.

- Hold your breath. This technique should help you relax in 30 seconds. Take a deep breath and keep it in. Holding palm to palm, press your fingers together. Wait 5 seconds, then slowly exhale through your lips while letting your hands relax. Do this five or six times until you unwind.

- Pay attention to such signs of stress as a tension headache and stop what you are doing for a rest break. If possible, take a warm bath or treat yourself to a massage during periods of stress. If this is not possible, practice deep abdominal breathing whenever you feel muscular tension setting in.

- Don't neglect your diet. Start off with a breakfast holding protein and carbohydrates for sustained energy and don't let the demands of your day get in the way of lunch.

- Take a ten-minute holiday: Meditation is a great stress reliever, but sometimes it's hard to find the time or place for it. Take a mini-holiday right at your desk or kitchen table instead. Just close your eyes, breathe deeply (from your stomach) and picture yourself lying on a beach the Gold Coast (Australia) or Hawaii. Feel the warmth of the sun. Hear the waves. Smell the salt air. Just put a little distance between yourself and your stress. A few minutes a day can be a major help.

- Keep it Quiet or Down: If you work, live or play in a high-noise area, consider wearing earplugs. Make sure the ones you buy reduce sound by at least 20 decibels.

Just remember when everything
Looks like turning to crap
Keep a positive attitude.

Also Remember, on their deathbed, no one says:

"I wish I'd spent more time at work"

I hope that my dreams and goals and how I achieve them will help you.

Thinking Positive, Positive Attitude,

Self-Esteem, Stay Focused, Learn to Say NO,

And your affirmations will realise your dreams and goals.

****

People Who Have Had an Influence on My Life
My Family:

Because they are just that, my rock and corner stone of my Life, always there no matter what the situation.

****

Mohammed Ali and Michael J Fox:

For their determination and endurance to overcome their battle with Parkinson's disease.

Dr John DeMartini:

He has inspired me from my first meeting, to go for

my dreams and aspire to whatever I want to be.

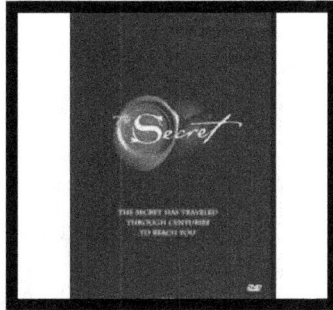

The Secret:

Second only to the Bible, as the most powerful

book known to mankind.

Rhonda Byrne:

The Author who brought us *'The Secret'* .

Mahatma Ghandi:

For being a leader for his people and the down

Trodden of the world.

Sir Edmund Hillary and Tensing Norgay:
For conquering what the world said could not
be carried out.

Albert Einstein:
For the way he conquered his demons and
achieve his dreams.

Lady Diana:

For her humanity and love she shared with the world.

John F. Kennedy:

The greatest President the USA has had since Lincoln. His vision and foresight was illuminating to most. His assassination was the end of an era.

Abraham Lincoln:

He said, *"Everyman has the right to Freedom."*

Martin Luther King Jr.:

'He Had a Dream', which due to his assassination never came to fruition.

Reverend Desmond Tutu:

For his enduring fight against Apartheid and inhumanity

Nelson Mandela:

He is an inspiration for his beliefs and knowing his dream was to free his beloved South Africa

Mark Twain:

Made the world so simplified with his writings and

philosophy.

Sigmund Freud
Father of Psychoanalysis

Napoleon Hill:
He showed us how to *"Think and Grow Rich"*

Do not let anything clutter your mind, Time is on your side but outside influences can stop you

achieving your dreams.

About The Author

Born in Australia, graduated from High School and spent most of my teenage life and early twenties in the Royal Australian Air Force. I have a Degree in Psychology, Education, and a Post Graduate Degrees in Human Sciences, Behaviour and Health as well as a Degree in Teaching. I investigate and specialise in Criminal and Forensic Psychology as well as Human behaviour. I do not practice or work now but I have worked in many areas. I am married and settled in New Zealand.
I have three grown children and a grandchild. I am a family man, first and foremost. Hobbies are golf, fishing, reading and being an author. I started writing at 32; I never really wanted to publish anything but did Self-Publish three books in 2008. Of the three books; two were Non-Fiction and a Self Help Book. I also have a book that is the first adventure into full Psychological Crime Fiction, taking almost two years to complete. I write when something inspires me for the ideas to flow. Have read many works from varied authors and believe we can never read or learn too much.
My favourite quote is: "We are placed on this earth for a purpose, and the three most important things in life are the day you were born, why you were born, and the day you die".
My biggest inspirations: are family, friends, and the larger Universe of Life.